Jack C. Richards & Chuck Sandy

Passages

Third Edition

Student's Book
with eBook

2A

CAMBRIDGE
UNIVERSITY PRESS

CAMBRIDGE
UNIVERSITY PRESS

University Printing House, Cambridge CB2 8BS, United Kingdom

One Liberty Plaza, 20th Floor, New York, NY 10006, USA

477 Williamstown Road, Port Melbourne, VIC 3207, Australia

314–321, 3rd Floor, Plot 3, Splendor Forum, Jasola District Centre, New Delhi – 110025, India

103 Penang Road, #05-06/07, Visioncrest Commercial, Singapore 238467

Cambridge University Press is part of the University of Cambridge.

It furthers the University's mission by disseminating knowledge in the pursuit of education, learning and research at the highest international levels of excellence.

www.cambridge.org
Information on this title: www.cambridge.org/9781009040846

First published 1998
Second edition 2008
Reprinted 2019
Third edition 2015
Update to Third edition published 2021

20 19 18 17 16 15 14 13 12 11 10 9 8 7 6 5 4 3 2

Printed in Poland by Opolgraf

A catalogue record for this publication is available from the British Library

ISBN 978-1-009-04083-9 Student's Book 2 with eBook
ISBN 978-1-009-04084-6 Student's Book 2A with eBook
ISBN 978-1-009-04085-3 Student's Book 2B with eBook
ISBN 978-1-009-04092-1 Student's Book 2 with Digital Pack
ISBN 978-1-009-04093-8 Student's Book 2A with Digital Pack
ISBN 978-1-009-04094-5 Student's Book 2B with Digital Pack
ISBN 978-1-107-62726-0 Workbook 2
ISBN 978-1-107-62734-5 Workbook 2A
ISBN 978-1-107-62780-2 Workbook 2B
ISBN 978-1-107-62766-6 Teacher's Edition 2 with Assessment Audio
ISBN 978-1-107-62749-9 Class Audio 2
ISBN 978-1-009-04095-2 Full Contact 2 with Digital Pack
ISBN 978-1-009-04096-9 Full Contact 2A with Digital Pack
ISBN 978-1-009-04097-6 Full Contact 2B with Digital Pack
ISBN 978-1-107-62764-2 DVD 2
ISBN 978-1-107-68650-2 Presentation Plus 2

Additional resources for this publication at cambridgeone.org

Art direction, book design, layout services, and photo research: Q2A / Bill Smith
Audio production: John Marshall Media
Video production: Steadman Productions

Authors' Acknowledgments

A great number of people contributed to the development of *Passages Third Edition*. Particular thanks are owed to the following reviewers and institutions, as their insights and suggestions have helped define the content and format of the third edition:

Paulo A. Machado, Rio de Janeiro, Brazil; Simone C. Wanguestel, Niterói, Brazil; Athiná Arcadinos Leite, **ACBEU**, Salvador, Brazil; Lauren Osowski, **Adult Learning Center**, Nashua, NH, USA; Brenda Victoria, **AIF System**, Santiago, Dominican Republic; Alicia Mitchell-Boncquet, **ALPS Language School**, Seattle, WA, USA; Scott C. Welsh, **Arizona State University**, Tempe, AZ, USA; Silvia Corrêa, **Associação Alumni**, São Paulo, Brazil; Henrick Oprea, **Atlantic Idiomas**, Brasília, Brazil; Márcia Lima, **B.A. English School**, Goiânia, Brazil; Carlos Andrés Mejía Gómez, **BNC Centro Colombo Americano Pereira**, Pereira, Colombia; Tanja Jakimoska, **Brava Training**, Rio de Janeiro, Brazil; Paulo Henrique Gomes de Abreu, **Britannia International English**, Rio de Janeiro, Brazil; Gema Kuri Rodríguez, **Business & English**, Puebla, Mexico; Isabela Villas Boas, **Casa Thomas Jefferson**, Brasília, Brazil; Inara Lúcia Castillo Couto, **CEL-LEP**, São Paulo, Brazil; Ana Cristina Hebling Meira, **Centro Cultural Brasil-Estados Unidos**, Campinas, Brazil; Juliana Costa da Silva, **Centro de Cultura Anglo Americana**, Rio de Janeiro, Brazil; Heriberto Díaz Vázquez, **Centro de Investigación y Docencia Económicas**, Mexico City, Mexico; D. L. Dorantes-Salas, **Centro de Investigaciones Biológicas del Noroeste**, La Paz, Mexico; Elizabeth Carolina Llatas Castillo, **Centro Peruano Americano El Cultural**, Trujillo-La Libertad, Peru; Márcia M. A. de Brito, **Chance Language Center**, Rio de Janeiro, Brazil; Rosalinda Heredia, **Colegio Motolinia**, San Juan del Río, Mexico; Maria Regina Pereira Filgueiras, **College Language Center**, Londrina, Brazil; Lino Mendoza Rodriguez, **Compummunicate**, Izúcar de Matamoros, Mexico; Maria Lucia Sciamarelli, **Cultura Inglesa**, Campinas, Brazil; Elisabete Thess, **Cultura Inglesa**, Petrópolis, Brazil; Catarina M. B. Pontes Kruppa, **Cultura Inglesa**, São Paulo, Brazil; Sheila Lima, **Curso Oxford**, Rio de Janeiro, Brazil; Elaine Florencio, Beth Vasconcelos, **English House Corporate**, Rio de Janeiro, Brazil; Vasti Rodrigues e Silva, **Fox Idiomas**, Rio de Janeiro, Brazil; Ricardo Ramos Miguel Cézar, Walter Júnior Ribeiro Silva, **Friends Language Center**, Itapaci, Brazil; Márcia Maria Pedrosa Sá Freire de Souza, **IBEU**, Rio de Janeiro, Brazil; Jerusa Rafael, **IBEUV**, Vitória, Brazil; Lilianne de Souza Oliveira, **ICBEU**, Manaus, Brazil; Liviane Santana Paulino de Carvalho, **ICBEU**, São Luís, Brazil; Manuel Marrufo Vásquez, **iempac Instituto de Enseñanza del Idioma Ingles**, Tequila, Mexico; Nora Aquino, **Instituto de Ciencias y Humanidades Tabasco**, Villahermosa, Mexico; Andrea Grimaldo, **Instituto Laurens**, Monterrey, Mexico; Cenk Aykut, Staci Jenkins, Kristen Okada, **Interactive College of Technology**, Chamblee, GA, USA; Imeen Manahan-Vasquez, Zuania Serrano, **Interactive Learning Systems**, Pasadena, TX, USA; Nicholas J. Jackson, **Jackson English School**, Uruapan, Mexico; Marc L. Cummings, **Jefferson Community and Technical College**, Louisville, KY, USA; Solange Nery Veloso, **Nery e Filho Idiomas**, Rio de Janeiro, Brazil; Tomas Sparano Martins, **Phil Young's English School**, Curitiba, Brazil; Paulo Cezar Lira Torres, **PRIME Language Center**, Vitória, Brazil; Angie Vasconcellos, **Robin English School**, Petrópolis, Brazil; Barbara Raifsnider, **San Diego Community College District**, San Diego, CA, USA; James Drury de Matos Fonseca, **SENAC**, Fortaleza, Brazil; Manoel Fialho da Silva Neto, **SENAC**, Recife, Brazil; Marilyn Ponder, **Tecnológico de Monterrey**, Irapuato, Mexico; Linda M. Holden, **The College of Lake County**, Grayslake, IL, USA; Janaína da Silva Cardoso, **UERJ**, Rio de Janeiro, Brazil; Gustavo Reges Ferreira, Sandlei Moraes de Oliveira, **UFES**, Vitória, Brazil; Nancy Alarcón Mendoza, **UNAM, Facultad de Estudios Superiores Zaragoza**, Mexico City, Mexico; Rosa Awilda López Fernández, **UNAPEC**, Santo Domingo, Dominican Republic; Vera Lúcia Ratide, **Unilínguas**, São Leopoldo, Brazil; Elsa Yolanda Cruz Maldonado, **Universidad Autónoma de Chiapas**, Tapachula, Mexico; Deida Perea, **Universidad Autónoma de Ciudad Juárez**, Ciudad Juárez, Mexico; Gabriela Ladrón de Guevara de León, **Universidad Autónoma de la Ciudad de México**, Mexico City, Mexico; Juan Manuel Ardila Prada, **Universidad Autónoma de Occidente**, Cali, Colombia; Lizzete G. Acosta Cruz, **Universidad Autónoma de Zacatecas**, Fresnillo, Mexico; Ary Guel, Fausto Noriega, Areli Martínez Suaste, **Universidad Autónoma de Zacatecas**, Zacatecas, Mexico; Gabriela Cortés Sánchez, **Universidad Autónoma Metropolitana Azcapotzalco**, Mexico City, Mexico; Secundino Isabeles Flores, Guillermo Guadalupe Duran Garcia, Maria Magdalena Cass Zubiria, **Universidad de Colima**, Colima, Mexico; Alejandro Rodríguez Sánchez, **Universidad del Golfo de México Norte**, Orizaba, Mexico; Fabiola Meneses Argüello, **Universidad La Salle Cancún**, Cancún, Mexico; Claudia Isabel Fierro Castillo, **Universidad Politécnica de Chiapas**, Tuxtla Gutierrez, Mexico; Eduardo Aguirre Rodríguez, M.A. Carolina Labastida Villa, **Universidad Politécnica de Quintana Roo**, Cancún, Mexico; Gabriela de Jesús Aubry González, **Universidad TecMilenio Campus Veracruz**, Boca del Rio, Mexico; Frank Ramírez Marín, **Universidad Veracruzana**, Boca del Río, Mexico.

Additional thanks are owed to Alex Tilbury for revising the Self-assessment charts, Paul MacIntyre for revising the Grammar Plus section, and Karen Kawaguchi for writing the Vocabulary Plus section.

Welcome to **Passages!**

Congratulations! You have learned the basics; now it's time to raise your English to a whole new level.

Your journey through each unit of ***Passages Third Edition*** will include a range of activities that will **progressively expand your language ability** in a variety of contexts, including formal and informal communication.

Along the way, you will encounter frequent communication reviews and progress checks that will **systematically consolidate your learning**, while **additional grammar and vocabulary practice** is available whenever you need it in the Grammar Plus and Vocabulary Plus sections in the back of this book.

RAISING YOUR ENGLISH TO A WHOLE NEW LEVEL

Unique features to boost your English proficiency!

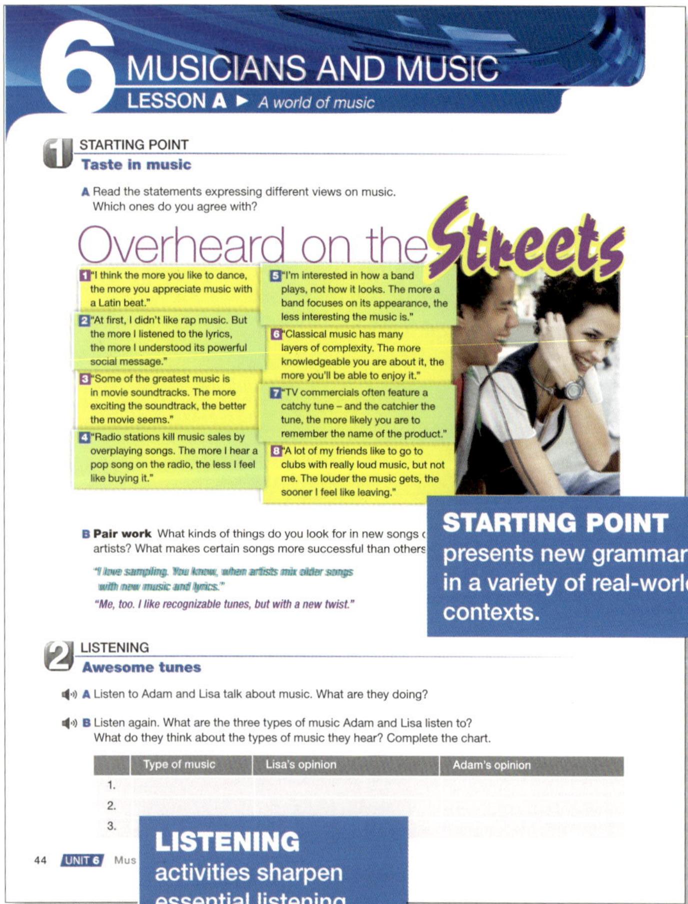

6 MUSICIANS AND MUSIC

LESSON A ► *A world of music*

1 STARTING POINT

Taste in music

A Read the statements expressing different views on music. Which ones do you agree with?

Overheard on the Streets

1 "I think the more you like to dance, the more you appreciate music with a Latin beat."

2 "At first, I didn't like rap music. But the more I listened to the lyrics, the more I understood its powerful social message."

3 "Some of the greatest music is in movie soundtracks. The more exciting the soundtrack, the better the movie seems."

4 "Radio stations kill music sales by overplaying songs. The more I hear a pop song on the radio, the less I feel like buying it."

5 "I'm interested in how a band plays, not how it looks. The more a band focuses on its appearance, the less interesting the music is."

6 "Classical music has many layers of complexity. The more knowledgeable you are about it, the more you'll be able to enjoy it."

7 "TV commercials often feature a catchy tune – and the catchier the tune, the more likely you are to remember the name of the product."

8 "A lot of my friends like to go to clubs with really loud music, but not me. The louder the music gets, the sooner I feel like leaving."

B Pair work What kinds of things do you look for in new songs or artists? What makes certain songs more successful than others?

"I love sampling. You know, when artists mix older songs with new music and lyrics."

"Me, too. I like recognizable tunes, but with a new twist."

2 LISTENING

Awesome tunes

A Listen to Adam and Lisa talk about music. What are they doing?

B Listen again. What are the three types of music Adam and Lisa listen to? What do they think about the types of music they hear? Complete the chart.

	Type of music	Lisa's opinion	Adam's opinion
1.			
2.			
3.			

44 UNIT 6 Mus

STARTING POINT
presents new grammar in a variety of real-world contexts.

LISTENING
activities sharpen essential listening comprehension skills.

GRAMMAR
is explored in context and builds on previously encountered structures.
Grammar Plus:
extra grammar explanations and practice when you need it!

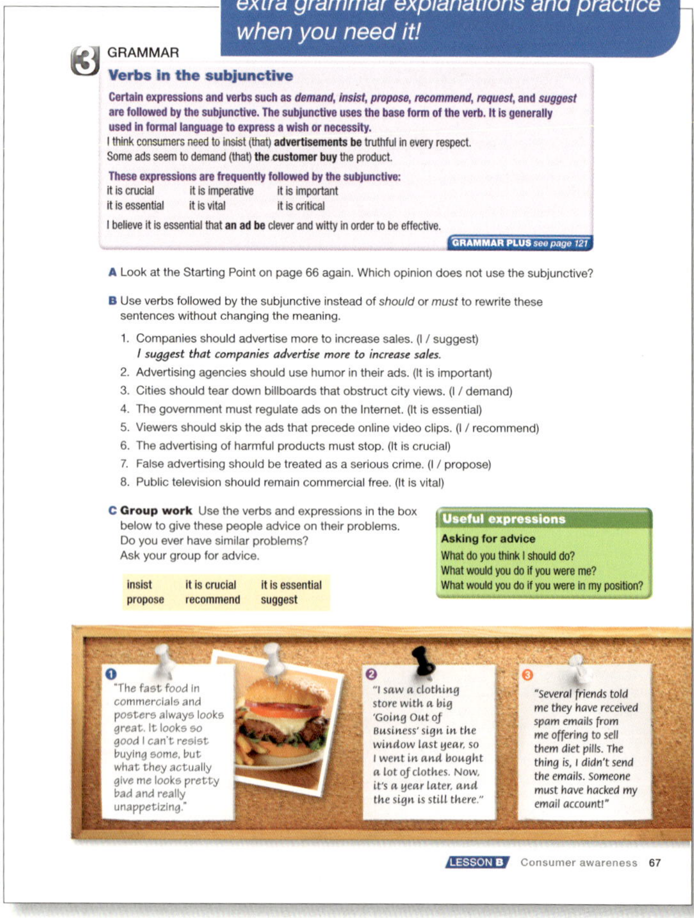

3 GRAMMAR

Verbs in the subjunctive

Certain expressions and verbs such as *demand, insist, propose, recommend, request,* and *suggest* are followed by the subjunctive. The subjunctive uses the base form of the verb. It is generally used in formal language to express a wish or necessity.

I think consumers need to insist (that) **advertisements be** truthful in every respect.

Some ads seem to demand (that) **the customer buy** the product.

These expressions are frequently followed by the subjunctive:

it is crucial — it is imperative — it is important
it is essential — it is vital — it is critical

I believe it is essential that **an ad be** clever and witty in order to be effective.

GRAMMAR PLUS see page 121

A Look at the Starting Point on page 66 again. Which opinion does not use the subjunctive?

B Use verbs followed by the subjunctive instead of *should* or *must* to rewrite these sentences without changing the meaning.

1. Companies should advertise more to increase sales. (I / suggest)
   I suggest that companies advertise more to increase sales.
2. Advertising agencies should use humor in their ads. (It is important)
3. Cities should tear down billboards that obstruct city views. (I / demand)
4. The government must regulate ads on the Internet. (It is essential)
5. Viewers should skip the ads that precede online video clips. (I / recommend)
6. The advertising of harmful products must stop. (It is crucial)
7. False advertising should be treated as a serious crime. (I / propose)
8. Public television should remain commercial free. (It is vital)

C Group work Use the verbs and expressions in the box below to give these people advice on their problems. Do you ever have similar problems? Ask your group for advice.

insist	it is crucial	it is essential
propose	recommend	suggest

Useful expressions

Asking for advice

What do you think I should do?
What would you do if you were me?
What would you do if you were in my position?

1 "The fast food in commercials and posters always looks great. It looks so good I can't resist buying some, but what they actually give me looks pretty bad and really unappetizing."

2 "I saw a clothing store with a big 'Going Out of Business' sign in the window last year, so I went in and bought a lot of clothes. Now, it's a year later, and the sign is still there."

3 "Several friends told me they have received spam emails from me offering to sell them diet pills. The thing is, I didn't send the emails. Someone must have hacked my email account!"

LESSON B Consumer awareness 67

VOCABULARY
expands upon prior knowledge and improves vocabulary building skills.
NEW *Vocabulary Plus:*
extra vocabulary practice when you need it!

4 VOCABULARY & SPEAKING
Different attitudes

A Look at these expressions. Which ones express a positive atti[…] attitude, or a neutral attitude? Write +, –, or ~.

___ 1. aware of
___ 2. curious about
___ 3. sick of
___ 4. fed up with
___ 5. familiar with
___ 6. suspicious of
___ 7. intimidated by
___ 8. knowledgeable abou[…]

B Group work Look at the list of inventions and technologies. […] What are your feelings about them? Discuss with your group.

1. spacecraft for private flights
2. touch-screen technology
3. speech-translation technology
4. video surveillance
5. wearable electronics
6. mobile apps
7. laser surgery
8. robots

"So, what do you think about spacecraft for private flights?"
"I'm a little intimidated by the idea of being in space. I'm curious about it, but I wouldn't try it."

VOCABULARY PLUS see page 132

5 DISCUSSION
Tech savvy?

A Are you a technophile or a technophobe? Complete the survey to find out.

TECHNOPHILE or TECHNOPHOBE? Agree (2 pts.) | Not Sure (1 pt.) | Disagree (0 pts.)

1. If technology permits it, I would favor the development of […] machines that surpass humans in intelligence.
2. Governments need to generously fund research and development in technology.
3. Everyone should try to stay informed about the latest innovations in technology.
4. Genetic technologies should be used to gradually improv[…] the human body over the course of generations.
5. Science and technology will someday solve the world's problems of famine, war, disease, and overcrowding.
6. It's important to acquire new technological devices short[…] after they come out.
7. Social media has a positive effect on people's social live[…]
8. Being connected to the Internet is a human right.

SCORE
0–4 You are a technophobe, a person who has a strong mistrust of technology.
5–8 While not in love with technology, you see the need for it in our world.

B Group work Discuss your answers to the survey. Ta[…] your choices and whether or not you agree with your […]

24

SPEAKING
activities spark lively discussions focusing on interesting and relevant situations.

6 WRITING
Compare-and-contrast essays

A compare-and-contrast essay presents the similarities and differences of two or more things. The thesis statement expresses your position on the subject, and it is followed by supporting paragraphs that discuss similarities and differences.

A Read the essay and circle the thesis statement. Then match each paragraph to the headings below. Underline the words that show[…]

___ introduction ___ differences ___ co[…]

1 Although the Beatles and the Rolling Stones have both been called the "greatest rock 'n' roll band of all time," the prize should go to the Rolling Stones. While both bands have had a huge influence on popular music, the Beatles broke up in 1970, and the Rolling Stones went on recording and performing for over 50 years.

2 Both the Beatles and the Rolling Stones began as four-member British bands that first became popular in the 1960s. The two bands released their first records within a year of each other, and both featured a pair of talented songwriters: Paul McCartney and John Lennon for the Beatles, and Mick Jagger and Keith Richards for the Rolling Stones. Like the Rolling Stones, the Beatles were famous for their cutting-edge style at the time of their debut, and both bands were known for their energetic stage performances.

B Choose two bands, singers, or musical styles to c[…] make a list of similarities and differences. Then co[…] that expresses your view.

C Write a four-paragraph essay. Make sure it has an […] thesis statement, two paragraphs describing simila[…] an effective conclusion.

D Pair work Take turns reading your essays. Do no[…] Can your partner guess your point of view?

WRITING
tasks build academic writing skills through step-by-step activities.

Passages Third Edition is a two-level course that will open the door to communicating with greater fluency and proficiency, with:

- **more sophisticated** real-world grammar and vocabulary,
- **thought-provoking** discussions and academic writing activities,
- **more challenging** listening and reading comprehension topics.

READING
passages drawn from authentic sources promote critical thinking and analysis.

6 READING
Technology and friendship

A Pair work Discuss these questions. Then read the article to compare your ideas with the author's.

1. What are some ways that interacting online might encourage people to connect in real life?
2. How could social media help shy students participate more in class?

HOW SOCIAL MEDIA "FRIENDS" TRANSLATE INTO REAL-LIFE FRIENDSHIPS

When social media first gained attention, I heard many people say online connections couldn't possibly be real friends. Some even feared people might trade face-to-face interaction for a virtual life online. But now the majority of the people I know consider at least some of their online friends to be like extended family. Which made me wonder – does social media actually encourage people to connect "in real life"?

One example of online life translating into real-life interaction happens on *Mashable*'s Social Media Day, when thousands of people attend in-person meet-ups to celebrate the power of online connections. Another example is location-based apps that help users connect face-to-face by allowing them to see who else has checked in at the same store, restaurant, or party – or even who is living in a city they plan to visit. They might then decide to seek each other out "in real life."

A Pew Internet and American Life Project report found that people using social networking sites have more close relationships and receive more support than others. They are also more likely to reconnect with old friends and use social networking to keep up with those they are already close to.

Other research shows that social media may also deepen what could otherwise be passing relationships. A study by Dr. Rey Junco found that college students who interacted with each other and their professors on Twitter were more likely to meet outside class to study. They also developed unexpected real-life connections and were also more likely to ask questions in class.

"What I find most fascinating is that I've consistently seen that students who start a course being more introverted and not speaking up during class discussions become more extroverted and participate more when encouraged to communicate through social media with their professors and their classmates," Junco said.

However, if social media does increase the likelihood of real-life interaction, it can also sometimes complicate it. When fans of social media meet face-to-face, their computers and mobile devices may actually make the meeting less productive. Instead of looking at each other, they may be glued to their screens!

Source: "How Social Media 'Friends' Translate Into Real-Life Friendships," by Terri Thornton, *Mediashift*

B Group work Discuss these questions. Then share your answers with the class.

1. In what ways are virtual friendships similar to and different from real-life friendships?
2. Would you be more or less willing to share ideas on social media than you would in class? Why?
3. What other issues and complications might come up when online friends meet face-to-face?

LESSON B Make new friends, but keep the old . . . 9

KEEP MOVING UP!
More support is always available – when and where you need it!

The **WORKBOOK** provides extensive practice of grammar and vocabulary as well as additional reading and writing activities.

The **DIGITAL WORKBOOK** – a digital version of the Workbook – enables your teacher to provide instant feedback on your work.

AUDIO AND VIDEO on Cambridge One allows students to review on their own.

cambridgeone.org

Plan of **BOOK 2A**

	FUNCTIONS	GRAMMAR	VOCABULARY
UNIT 1 Relationships pages 2–9			
A The best of friends **B** Make new friends, but keep the old . . .	▪ Defining and describing friendship ▪ Expressing opinions ▪ Disagreeing politely ▪ Stating preferences ▪ Sharing advice about friendship	▪ Phrasal verbs ▪ Gerund and infinitive constructions	▪ Adjectives and verbs to describe friendship ▪ *re-* verbs
UNIT 2 Clothes and appearance pages 10–17			
A The way we dress **B** How we appear to others	▪ Discussing approaches to fashion ▪ Describing style and trends ▪ Expressing opinions about clothing ▪ Talking about first impressions ▪ Describing outward appearance	▪ Review of verb patterns ▪ Cleft sentences with *what*	▪ Adjectives to describe style ▪ Adjectives to describe outward appearance
UNIT 3 Science and technology pages 18–25			
A Good science, bad science **B** Technology and you	▪ Talking about scientific advances ▪ Analyzing the effects of science and technology ▪ Expressing caution and confidence ▪ Describing technology troubles	▪ Indefinite and definite articles ▪ *-ing* clauses	▪ Adjectives to discuss technology-related issues ▪ Collocations to express different attitudes
UNITS 1–3 Communication review pages 26–27			
UNIT 4 Superstitions and beliefs pages 28–35			
A Superstitions **B** Believe it or not	▪ Talking about personal beliefs ▪ Comparing beliefs ▪ Reporting what other people believe ▪ Expressing opinions	▪ Reporting clauses ▪ Reporting clauses in the passive	▪ Expressions with *luck* ▪ Adjectives to describe truth and fabrication
UNIT 5 Movies and television pages 36–43			
A Movies **B** Television	▪ Discussing movie trends ▪ Expressing your attitude about trends ▪ Discussing movie genre aspects and preferences ▪ Discussing TV show preferences ▪ Explaining the popularity of TV shows	▪ Sentence adverbs ▪ *Such . . . that* and *so . . . that*	▪ Adjectives to describe movies ▪ Types of TV programs
UNIT 6 Musicians and music pages 44–51			
A A world of music **B** Getting your big break	▪ Sharing views on music ▪ Expressing preferences ▪ Comparing and contrasting ▪ Defining success	▪ Double comparatives ▪ *Will* and *would* for habits and general truths	▪ Collocations to describe music ▪ Idioms used in the entertainment industry
UNITS 4–6 Communication review pages 52–53			
GRAMMAR PLUS: Additional grammar practice and explanation pages 106–117			
VOCABULARY PLUS: Additional vocabulary practice pages 130–135			

SPEAKING	LISTENING	WRITING	READING
■ Talking about what friends should have in common ■ Talking about the best way to meet people ■ Discussing ways to maintain friendships	■ A talk about differences between friendships among men and friendships among women ■ A young woman describes a chance encounter	■ Developing a thesis statement ■ Writing a composition with paragraphs supporting a thesis statement	■ "How Social Media 'Friends' Translate into Real-life Friendships": Does social media encourage people to connect in real life?
■ Discussing different opinions on fashion ■ Discussing how first impressions are formed ■ Discussing tips for making a good first impression ■ Discussing how people respond to appearance	■ Three people describe their taste in fashion ■ Three people explain what is important for them when forming an impression	■ Writing a composition about a personal belief ■ Giving examples to support a thesis statement	■ "Overcoming a Bad First Impression": How to change a bad first impression
■ Discussing the positive effects and negative consequences of technology and science ■ Discussing your feelings about new technology ■ Taking a survey about your relationship with technology	■ A reporter and technology editor talk about the impact of driverless car technology ■ A comedian talks about difficulties he has had with technology	■ Identifying essential information for a summary of a text ■ Writing a summary of an article	■ "I Took My Kids Offline": A mother bans all technology at home for six months
■ Describing superstitions from your country or culture ■ Discussing superstitions ■ Taking a survey about luck ■ Telling stories ■ Discussing hoaxes and why people create them	■ Three people give explanations for some superstitions ■ Two people discuss a journalistic hoax	■ Restating the thesis in the last paragraph ■ Writing a composition about superstitions	■ "Do Good Luck Charms Really Work in Competitions?": The effectiveness of superstitious rituals in sports
■ Talking about movie trends ■ Talking about the results of a survey on movie genre preferences ■ Discussing aspects of different movie genres ■ Discussing what makes a TV show popular ■ Discussing and presenting an idea for a new TV show	■ Four people describe what makes some movie genres effective ■ TV network employees brainstorm and present ideas for new TV shows	■ Identifying essential information for a movie review ■ Writing a movie review	■ "*One Day on Earth*: A Time Capsule of Our Lives": A movie shot in every country of the world on the same day
■ Talking about personal tastes in music ■ Talking about styles of music ■ Discussing the role of music in different contexts ■ Discussing advice for success	■ Two people share their opinions on different types of music ■ A young woman gives her friend advice on his music career	■ Writing a compare-and-contrast essay ■ Describing similarities and differences	■ "On the Trail of Sixto Rodriguez": Searching for a musician who was famous and didn't know it

1 RELATIONSHIPS

LESSON A ▶ *The best of friends*

1 STARTING POINT
The nature of friendship

A Read these statements about friendship. Can you explain what they mean? What other statements would you add to the list?

WHAT IS A Friend?

1. A friend is someone who brings out the best in you.
2. Good friends are always happy to help when you run into a problem.
3. A friend is someone who cheers you up when you're feeling bad.
4. True friends don't drift apart even after many years of separation.
5. A real friend will always stand up for you when others are putting you down.
6. Never be afraid to open up and ask a friend for advice. A true friend will never turn you down.
7. Make new friends, but hang on to the old ones.
8. Good friends are hard to come by, harder to leave, and impossible to do without.

"The first statement means a friend inspires you to show all your positive qualities."

B Group work Consider the statements in part A. What makes a good friend? Discuss with your group.

"In my opinion, a good friend is someone who makes you a better person. It's someone who brings out the best in you."

Useful expressions

Expressing opinions

In my opinion, . . .
I have to say that . . .
The way I see it, . . .
Personally, I (don't) think . . .

2 LISTENING & SPEAKING
Friendship among women and men

A Listen to a professor talk about author Deborah Tannen's ideas. In Tannen's opinion, what is the main difference between friendship among men and friendship among women?

B Listen again. According to Tannen, which of these things do male friends often do (*M*) and which do female friends often do (*F*)? Write the correct letter.

____ 1. are direct and to the point
____ 2. discuss daily life at length
____ 3. reveal private thoughts
____ 4. prefer to share factual information
____ 5. value activities over talk
____ 6. talk as a way to better understand their lives

C Group work Do you agree or disagree with Tannen's ideas about friendship? Why or why not?

"I have to say that I think some of her ideas seem to be accurate . . ."

3 GRAMMAR

Phrasal verbs

A phrasal verb is a verb plus a particle, such as *down*, *into*, *out*, or *up*.
The meaning of a phrasal verb is usually different from the meaning of its parts.

Separable phrasal verbs can take objects before or after the particle.
If the object is a pronoun, it always appears before the particle.
A friend is someone who **brings out** the best in you.
A friend is someone who **brings** the best **out** in you.
A friend is someone who **cheers** you **up** when you're feeling bad.

With inseparable phrasal verbs, the object cannot go between the verb and the particle.
Good friends are always happy to help when you **run into** a problem.

Three-word phrasal verbs have a particle and a preposition.
Make new friends, but **hang on to** the old ones.

Intransitive phrasal verbs don't take objects.
True friends don't **drift apart**.

GRAMMAR PLUS *see page 106*

A Look at the Starting Point on page 2 again. Can you find the phrasal verbs? Which are separable, inseparable, and/or three-word verbs? Which are also intransitive? Write them in the chart.

Separable	Inseparable	Three-word verbs	Intransitive

B Complete the questions with the phrasal verbs and objects in parentheses. Sometimes more than one answer is possible.

1. Have you ever had a friend who *brought out the worst /* *brought the worst out* (bring out / the worst) in you?
2. Have you ever ______________ (run into / a friend) that you hadn't seen in a long time?
3. Do you usually ______________ (stand up for / your friends) when other people criticize them?
4. Can you ______________ (do without / a cell phone) and still keep in touch with friends?
5. When friends ask you for a favor, do you usually say yes, or do you ______________ (turn down / them)?
6. Do you ______________ (hang on to / your old friends) or do you drift apart as time goes by?
7. Some people like to ______________ (put down / their friends) by insulting them. How would you feel if a friend did that to you?

C Pair work Discuss the questions in part B.

"Have you ever had a friend who brought out the worst in you?"
"Yeah, I once had a really messy roommate. She made me so angry."

4 VOCABULARY
Describing friendship

A Pair work Complete the chart with the correct parts of speech.

	Verb	Adjective		Verb	Adjective
1.	admire		4.	empathize	
2.		beneficial	5.	endure	
3.	clash		6.		harmonious

B Choose the word from the chart in part A that best replaces the boldfaced words. Compare answers with a partner.

1. Ryan and Tina work to keep their friendship ~~**free of conflict**~~ *harmonious*.
2. Sometimes their opinions **are very different**, but they still get along.
3. They work to make their friendship **valuable and constructive**.
4. Having the same background helps them **understand and identify** with each other.
5. Ryan and Tina **think very highly of** each other's accomplishments.
6. Their friendship will certainly **last a long time**.

VOCABULARY PLUS *see page 130*

5 DISCUSSION
What should friends have in common?

A Look at the statements about friendship below. Do you agree with the statements? Add a statement of your own.

PEOPLE . . .	**Agree**	**Disagree**
1. who are close in age empathize with each other better.	☐	☐
2. with similar social backgrounds have more harmonious friendships.	☐	☐
3. who have similar values and beliefs have stronger connections.	☐	☐
4. with similar personalities have the most enduring friendships.	☐	☐
5. benefit from having friends with the same educational background.	☐	☐
6. should only mingle with friends who have the same interests.	☐	☐
7. from different cultures often clash with each other.	☐	☐
8. ________________________________.	☐	☐

B Group work Share your opinions and explain your reasons.

"The way I see it, people who are close in age can empathize better with each other. They share many of the same experiences and understand each other."

"I see your point, but I don't think age is that important. If people like doing similar things, they can be good friends."

Useful expressions

Disagreeing politely

I see your point, but . . .
I see what you mean, but . . .
I'm not sure I agree.
Do you think so?

C Group work How many people agreed or disagreed with each statement? Report your findings to the class.

"Three of us agreed that friends who are close in age empathize with each other better . . ."

6 WRITING
Developing a thesis statement

The first paragraph of a composition contains a thesis statement, which presents the main idea. The remaining paragraphs each have a single focus expressed in a topic sentence that develops the thesis statement.

A Read the composition. Underline the thesis statement in the first paragraph.

B Match each of the other paragraphs with the phrase below that best summarizes its focus.

____ why we have a close friendship ____ what we have in common ____ how we are different

1 My best friend, Eva, and I are different in many ways, but we have one important thing in common – we love to travel. Whenever I have the urge to explore a new place, I can always count on Eva to go with me. Our friendship shows that people who are very different can still have similar interests.

2 The differences between Eva and me are significant. Eva is an artist who loves to take photographs and draw pictures of the interesting things she sees. I am a marketing representative for a pharmaceutical company and spend a lot of my time estimating sales figures. Eva is a very impulsive person, and I'm very organized. She's very quiet, but I'm a very talkative person who enjoys telling stories.

3 Eva and I are both adventurous and love traveling. We discovered this shortly after we met several years ago. One day we were talking about vacations, and we found we had both visited many of the same places. We immediately made a plan to go to a nearby historical city the following weekend.

4 Although we are quite different in many ways, Eva and I have become close over the years, and we now have a very special and enduring friendship. Every time we get together, we always have so much to talk about and have the best time. One reason for this is that we share a love of travel and adventure. The other reason is that our differences complement each other, so we always get along well whenever we travel together.

C Write a composition about a close friend. Then exchange your composition with a partner, and answer these questions.

1. What is the thesis statement? Underline it.
2. Does each paragraph have a single focus? Write the focus for each in the margin of the text.
3. What else would you like to know about your partner's friend? Ask at least two questions.

LESSON B ▶ *Make new friends, but keep the old . . .*

1 STARTING POINT
Meeting new people

A Read about how Yuan Lin, Brandon, and Jacob met new people. Which way of meeting people do you think is best?

Yuan Lin

"I decided to move to England last year. I felt really lonely at first. In fact, I regretted moving here. But I never gave up trying new things. Then, I saw an ad for a Chinese-English language exchange. It was a great way to meet cool people!"

Brandon

"I'd been planning to take a class, but was putting off enrolling. Well, last month I started taking a cooking class. I never expected to meet so many nice people! Some of us get together at each other's homes and practice what we learn. We've become really good friends!"

Jacob

"I didn't know many people at my new job, but I kept being invited by my co-workers to a lunchtime yoga class. I'm so glad I finally said yes! A couple of my colleagues play soccer, too, and they're considering starting a company team!"

"A language exchange is a great idea. You can meet people who are interested in languages and culture, so everyone already has something in common."

B **Group work** What other ways of meeting new people can you suggest to someone in these situations? Add another situation to the list.

Someone who . . .

- moved to a new neighborhood
- has little free time
- started a new job
- is very shy
- is over 65 years old
- ____________________

2 LISTENING
A chance meeting

A **Pair work** When was the last time you unexpectedly ran into someone you know? Tell your partner about your experience.

B Listen to Dena talk about how she met her friend Kate. Where were they when they first met? Where did they meet again?

C Listen again. Then answer the following questions.

1. Why were Dena and Kate going to Los Angeles?
2. What did Dena regret after she said good-bye to Kate?
3. How much time passed between their first and second meetings?
4. How did Samantha, the guest at the party, know Kate?

3 GRAMMAR

Gerund and infinitive constructions

These verbs are normally followed by a gerund: *appreciate, consider, enjoy, give up, keep, put off, suggest.*

They're **considering starting** a company team!

These verbs are normally followed by an infinitive: *ask, decide, expect, intend, need, refuse, seem, tend.*

I never **expected to meet** so many nice people!

These verbs are followed by either a gerund or an infinitive: *begin, bother, continue, hate, prefer, start.*

Last month I **started taking / to take** a cooking class.

Infinitives and gerunds can also occur in the passive voice. They follow the pattern subject + verb + *being / to be* + past participle.

I **kept being invited** by my co-workers to a lunchtime yoga class.

She **asked to be chosen** for the job.

GRAMMAR PLUS *see page 107*

A Look at the Starting Point on page 6 again. Can you find another verb followed by a gerund and another verb followed by an infinitive?

B Choose the correct form of the verbs. Sometimes both answers are possible.

Monday, March 18

I've never been a really popular guy. I'm the type of person who tends **1** *to have / having* one or two good friends rather than lots of acquaintances. Well, when I moved away from my hometown after getting a job in Denver, I really needed **2** *to make / making* some new friends. Because I'm shy, I considered **3** *to change / changing* my personality to become more outgoing. But that was very difficult for me. Just the same, I didn't give up **4** *to try / trying*. I decided **5** *to create / creating* a new image for myself. I bought myself some new shoes, new clothes, and I even got a new haircut and started **6** *to wear / wearing* contact lenses. However, it didn't seem **7** *to change / changing* anything. I was beginning to regret **8** *to leave / leaving* my hometown when, all of a sudden, I got a call from my old friend Jim. He was planning **9** *to move / moving* here pretty soon. He wanted some advice about finding an apartment in the city, and I suggested **10** *to share / sharing* an apartment with me. Well, he agreed! I really enjoy **11** *to have / having* someone to spend time with, and together we've made a lot of new friends.

Posted by DenverDan **2 COMMENTS**

C Pair work Complete these sentences with your own information, and add details. Then compare with a partner.

1. I don't like it when friends refuse . . .
   to do small favors for me, like lending me a book. It's so rude.
2. It can be annoying when friends expect . . .
3. I couldn't say no if a friend suggested . . .
4. When I'm with my good friends, I don't bother . . .

4 VOCABULARY
re- verbs

A Which word best completes these sentences? Write the correct letter.

a. rebuild c. reconnect e. rehash g. replace
b. recall d. redefine f. rekindle h. resurface

1. You can __f__ old friendships by sharing memories.
2. Don't ____ old arguments over and over.
3. People often ____ themselves, but they're essentially the same.
4. A close friend is impossible to ____.
5. Can you ____ the first time you met your best friend?
6. Friends you think are gone forever sometimes ____ unexpectedly.
7. Visit your hometown and ____ with your roots.
8. It takes time to ____ a damaged friendship.

B **Pair work** What other *re-* verbs do you know? How would you define them? Compare your list with a partner.

Recapture, reconsider, . . .

VOCABULARY PLUS *see page 130*

5 DISCUSSION
Friendship maintenance

A Look at these ideas for maintaining friendships. Choose three that you think are the most important.

Advice for Maintaining FRIENDSHIPS

- Praise your friends often and keep a positive, optimistic attitude when you're around them.
- Never betray a friend's trust – it can cause real resentment.
- Try to be completely honest with your friends at all times.
- Don't hold unkind words against a friend. Consider any problems he or she has that might be the cause of the hurtful words.
- Use social media to help you feel connected to friends but not to replace face time.
- Be a good listener and try to empathize with your friends.
- Respect your friends' point of view even when you disagree. Don't rehash old arguments.
- Watch out for "unhealthy" friendships. Sometimes it's better to end a friendship and move on with your life.

B **Group work** Tell your group which three pieces of advice you chose, and explain why. Then share any other ideas you have about maintaining friendships.

"Well, I think it's important to always be completely honest with your friends. If you aren't honest with your friends, they might not be honest with you."

Useful expressions

Agreeing on importance

Well, I think it's important . . .
Yeah, that's true, but even more important is . . .
And let's not forget . . .
You're right . . . is also quite important.

6 READING

Technology and friendship

A Pair work Discuss these questions. Then read the article to compare your ideas with the author's.

1. What are some ways that interacting online might encourage people to connect in real life?
2. How could social media help shy students participate more in class?

HOW SOCIAL MEDIA "FRIENDS" TRANSLATE INTO REAL-LIFE FRIENDSHIPS

When social media first gained attention, I heard many people say online connections couldn't possibly be real friends. Some even feared people might trade face-to-face interaction for a virtual life online. But now the majority of the people I know consider at least some of their online friends to be like extended family. Which made me wonder – does social media actually encourage people to connect "in real life"?

One example of online life translating into real-life interaction happens on *Mashable*'s Social Media Day, when thousands of people attend in-person meet-ups to celebrate the power of online connections. Another example is location-based apps that help users connect face-to-face by allowing them to see who else has checked in at the same store, restaurant, or party – or even who is living in a city they plan to visit. They might then decide to seek each other out "in real life."

A Pew Internet and American Life Project report found that people using social networking sites have more close relationships and receive more support than others. They are also more likely to reconnect with old friends and use social networking to keep up with those they are already close to.

Other research shows that social media may also deepen what could otherwise be passing relationships. A study by Dr. Rey Junco found that college students who interacted with each other and their professors on Twitter were more likely to meet outside class to study. They also developed unexpected real-life connections and were also more likely to ask questions in class.

"What I find most fascinating is that I've consistently seen that students who start a course being more introverted and not speaking up during class discussions become more extroverted and participate more when encouraged to communicate through social media with their professors and their classmates," Junco said.

However, if social media does increase the likelihood of real-life interaction, it can also sometimes complicate it. When fans of social media meet face-to-face, their computers and mobile devices may actually make the meeting less productive. Instead of looking at each other, they may be glued to their screens!

Source: "How Social Media 'Friends' Translate Into Real-Life Friendships," by Terri Thornton, *Mediashift*

B Group work Discuss these questions. Then share your answers with the class.

1. In what ways are virtual friendships similar to and different from real-life friendships?
2. Would you be more or less willing to share ideas on social media than you would in class? Why?
3. What other issues and complications might come up when online friends meet face-to-face?

2 CLOTHES AND APPEARANCE

LESSON A ► *The way we dress*

1 STARTING POINT
Fashion sense

A What's your approach to fashion? Complete this survey.

Clothing Survey

	Agree	Disagree
1 When I choose clothes, I tend to think of comfort first and appearance second.	☐	☐
2 I hate choosing my outfits in the morning. I just put on anything I can find.	☐	☐
3 Celebrities sometimes inspire me to change the way I look.	☐	☐
4 Companies should discourage employees from wearing casual clothes to work.	☐	☐
5 I don't like to draw attention to myself, so I wear pretty conventional clothes.	☐	☐
6 I enjoy shopping for clothes. I don't mind spending hours in clothing stores.	☐	☐
7 High prices rarely prevent me from buying quality clothing.	☐	☐
8 Peer pressure sometimes compels me to wear brand-name clothing.	☐	☐

B Group work Discuss your answers to the survey.

"I tend to think of comfort first when I choose clothes. When I'm comfortable, I feel good, and that's more important to me than looking good."

2 DISCUSSION
Judging by appearances

A Pair work Read these famous quotations. In your own words, explain to a partner what they mean. Do you agree with the quotations?

It's always the badly dressed people who are the most interesting.
– Jean Paul Gaultier

You're never fully dressed without a smile.
– Martin Charnin

Three-tenths of good looks are due to nature; seven-tenths to dress.
– Chinese proverb

"I think the first one means interesting people focus on more meaningful things than clothes. I think it's often true. For example, scientists and inventors don't always dress very well."

B Group work Discuss these questions. Explain your answers.

1. Do you think it's fair for people to judge you by the way you dress?
2. If you had an unlimited clothing budget, would you change your style?
3. Would you change the way you dress to please someone else?

3 GRAMMAR

Review of verb patterns

Study the following common verb patterns.

a. verb + infinitive
When I choose clothes, I **tend to think** of comfort first and appearance second.

b. verb + object + infinitive
Celebrities sometimes **inspire me to change** the way I look.

c. verb + gerund
I **hate choosing** my outfits in the morning.

d. verb + object + preposition + gerund
High prices rarely **prevent me from buying** quality clothing.

GRAMMAR PLUS *see page 108*

A Look at the Starting Point on page 10 again. Can you find another example of each verb pattern above?

B Pair work Which verb patterns from the box do these sentences follow? Write *a*, *b*, *c*, or *d*.

____ 1. I enjoy making a statement with my clothes.
____ 2. I like to wear unusual color combinations.
____ 3. I refuse to shop with my friends.
____ 4. I can't help being critical of what others wear.
____ 5. Parents should allow their children to wear whatever they want.
____ 6. My friends usually advise me against spending too much on clothes.
____ 7. My parents have always discouraged me from wearing sloppy clothes.
____ 8. Advertising definitely convinces me to buy certain articles of clothing.

C Pair work Which statements above are true for you? Explain and give examples.

D Pair work Complete each sentence with a verb from the box and your own ideas. Then add a follow-up comment, and compare with a partner.

advise	discourage	encourage	require	tend
allow	don't mind	permit	seem	try

1. Some schools *require* students to wear *school uniforms*. *They think that students will spend more time studying and less time thinking about clothes.*
2. Parents often ________________ their children from ________________.
3. Some restaurants don't ________________ customers to ________________.
4. I ________________ to wear clothes that ________________.
5. Experts ________________ people against wearing ________________.
6. My clothes always ________________ to make me look ________________.
7. I ________________ buying expensive ________________.
8. Young people ________________ to be concerned about ________________.

4 VOCABULARY
Your taste in clothes

A Look at the words below. Do some have similar meanings? Which ones would you use to describe your own style?

chic	conservative	fashionable	formal	functional	quirky	sloppy	stylish
classic	elegant	flashy	frumpy	funky	retro	stuffy	trendy

B Pair work What do you think of these styles? Describe the people in the picture.

"Erica's outfit is pretty functional. She's probably going to the gym."
"Yes, but I'd say it's fashionable, too. The colors and design are stylish, and it fits her well."

VOCABULARY PLUS *see page 131*

5 LISTENING
Fashion developments

A Pair work Was your style the same five years ago? In what ways has your style changed? In what ways has it remained the same?

B Listen to Mark, Shelby, and Carlos describe how their tastes in fashion have changed. What was their style, and what is their style now?

	Then	Now
1. Mark		
2. Shelby		
3. Carlos		

C Listen again. Write the items of clothing or accessories you hear for each of the looks below.

grunge ______________________ bohemian ______________________
urban ______________________ sporty ______________________
goth ______________________ preppy ______________________

6 WRITING
Writing about personal beliefs

In a composition about a personal belief, clearly state that belief in a thesis statement in the first paragraph. In the following paragraphs, give examples to support your thesis.

A Look at these fashion mottos. Which motto best reflects your opinion about fashion? Why? Share your ideas with a partner.

Don't just get dressed. Make a statement.

Why look like everyone else?

Feel comfortable. That's all that matters.

Don't live in the past. Wear today's styles!

B Use the motto you chose as the basis for a thesis statement about your personal belief about fashion. Compare your ideas with a partner.

Your clothes should make a statement about who you are.

C Use your thesis statement to develop a composition of about 200 words in three paragraphs that describes your approach to clothes.

I believe that clothes should be more than functional. They should make a statement about who you are. Before you get dressed or go shopping for clothing, it's important to think about what kind of message your clothes will send to others.

I think of my clothes as a reflection of my personality. When people look at me and my clothes, they can get an idea of the kind of person I am. I'm interested in the arts, and I'm concerned about environmental issues. Therefore, I not only wear colorful clothes that are a bit unusual, but I also wear natural fabrics that are made locally. This is important to me.

I don't follow trends because I don't like to look like everyone else. I'm unique, and I want my clothes to show it.

D Pair work Exchange compositions and answer these questions.

1. Does the thesis statement in the first paragraph clearly state the writer's point of view?
2. Do the examples given in the other paragraphs support the thesis statement and clarify the writer's point of view?
3. What else do you want to know about your partner's attitude toward clothes?

LESSON B ▶ *How we appear to others*

1 STARTING POINT
Forming an impression

A Look at the statements about how people form a first impression of someone. Choose the statements that are true for you.

First Impressions
What People Notice First When They Meet Someone New

- ☐ What I notice is the other person's eyes.
- ☐ What's really important to me is a person's smile.
- ☐ What I always notice is a person's hands.
- ☐ I look at people's clothes first.
- ☐ What I notice is a person's figure (or physique).
- ☐ What strikes me first is the way people wear their hair.
- ☐ I always appreciate a nice pair of shoes.
- ☐ I have no idea what I notice first.

B Group work What other traits help you form an impression of a person? What are the three most important traits for the people in your group? Are they the same for men and women?

2 LISTENING
Important traits

A Listen to Gabriela, Joon, and Alice talk about what is important to them when forming an impression. Complete the chart.

	What is important
1. Gabriela	
2. Joon	
3. Alice	

B Listen again. Which speakers mention what is *not* very important to them? What do they mention? Complete the chart.

	What is not very important
1. Gabriela	
2. Joon	
3. Alice	

C Pair work Which speaker thinks the most like you? Share your reasons with a partner.

3 GRAMMAR

Cleft sentences with *what*

You can add *what* and a form of *be* to a sentence when you want to emphasize information. The resulting sentence is called a *cleft* sentence.

A person's smile **is really important to me.** — **What's really important to me is** a person's smile.

For sentences with verbs other than *be*, insert *what* at the beginning of the sentence and a form of *be* after the main verb.

I always notice a person's hands. — **What I always notice is** a person's hands.

GRAMMAR PLUS *see page 109*

A Look at the Starting Point on page 14 again. Can you find more cleft sentences? Try to change them into declarative sentences.

B Rewrite these sentences to add emphasis by beginning them with *what*. Which statements are true for you? Compare answers with a partner.

1. I appreciate a person with a good sense of humor.
   What I appreciate is a person with a good sense of humor.
2. I always notice the way people look at me.
3. A person's fashion sense is important to me.
4. I pay attention to people's manners.
5. I really dislike sarcasm.
6. I'm interested in the subjects people talk about.
7. A kind face is appealing to me.

4 DISCUSSION

Good first impressions

A Pair work Read these tips on making a good first impression. Choose the tip you think is the most useful. Then explain your choice to a partner.

QUICK TIPS for Making a Lasting Impression

1. Appearance matters. Dress a little nicer than you need to when meeting new people.
2. Occasionally, use the names of the people you are talking to, for example: *Amy, have you seen that movie yet?*
3. Break the silence with small talk about a topic that you think will interest others.
4. When it's in good taste, use humor. A joke can be a nice way to break the ice, but what you should avoid is sarcasm.
5. Everyone likes compliments, so give plenty of them. Just make sure you are sincere.
6. Be yourself, and be sure to smile. A friendly smile can make other people feel at ease.

B Group work What's the best way to make a good first impression in these situations? Discuss and add some tips of your own.

- a dinner party at a new friend's home
- an initial interview for a job you want
- the first day in a fitness class
- the first time you meet new neighbors

"At a dinner party with new friends, what's really important is good table manners."
"That's true. Also, what I always do is compliment my hosts on the food."

5 VOCABULARY
Adjectives to describe outward appearance

A Which adjectives seem to have a positive meaning, a negative meaning, or both? Write +, –, or +/–.

____ a. arrogant	____ d. innocent	____ g. sinister	____ i. sympathetic
____ b. dignified	____ e. intense	____ h. smug	____ j. trustworthy
____ c. eccentric	____ f. intellectual		

B Now match the words with their definitions. Write the correct letter.

1. rational and studious ____
2. kind and understanding ____
3. worthy of respect or honor ____
4. reliable ____
5. forceful; with strong opinions ____
6. proud in an unpleasant way ____
7. self-satisfied; pleased with oneself ____
8. without blame; childlike and pure ____
9. strange or unusual in an amusing way ____
10. evil or ominous ____

C **Pair work** What famous people do you think the adjectives describe?

"To me, Johnny Depp looks intellectual."

"Oh, I don't know. He looks eccentric, in my opinion."

VOCABULARY PLUS *see page 131*

6 DISCUSSION
Faces matter

Gisele Bündchen

John Cho

Psychologist Leslie Zebrowitz found that people are usually categorized by their faces. She gave résumés of equally qualified people to groups of business students, with photos attached. It was discovered that the students recommended baby-faced people for jobs that required more sympathetic and submissive people, while people with mature faces were seen as more dignified or intense and were recommended for high-powered jobs, like lawyers. "We found that the more baby-faced people had baby-faced jobs," Zebrowitz said. "People seemed to be chosen for jobs, or to select themselves into jobs, to match their appearance."

Source: "Judging Faces Comes Naturally," by Jules Crittenden, *Boston Herald*

Zooey Deschanel

Elijah Wood

Group work Answer these questions.

1. Which of the people above do you think have "baby faces"? What makes a baby face different from a mature face?
2. In what ways can having a baby face be useful? In what situations is it better to have a mature face?
3. In some countries, job applications sometimes require a recent photo of the candidate. Do you agree with this practice? Why or why not?

7 READING

Changing a negative perception

A Pair work In what ways could someone make a bad first impression? Once a bad impression is made, what can be done to change the negative perception? Discuss with a partner. Then read the article.

OVERCOMING A BAD FIRST IMPRESSION

Have any of these situations happened to you? Forgetting someone's name after you've just met, spilling coffee on your potential boss during an interview, or unintentionally insulting a co-worker on your first day? Ouch! You never have a second chance to make a first impression, so what happens when that first impression is a negative one? Here is how you can recover.

Apologize immediately. As soon as you realize that you may have offended someone, address it. The more time that passes, the more the story can become blown out of proportion. While first impressions stick, so do last impressions. Take control of the situation by making your last impression a positive one.

Avoid over-apologizing. Saying you're sorry is important, but overdoing it can create another uncomfortable situation. Your goal is to acknowledge your mistake and re-position yourself as being responsible and sensitive. If you repeatedly bring up the past, groveling and begging for forgiveness, you're defeating your purpose. It puts the other person in the uncomfortable position of having to constantly reassure you.

Make no assumptions. It's easy to assume that others think the worst of you, but usually what we imagine is far worse than reality. So, don't start out with, "You must think I'm a total idiot." Say something like, "I'm uncomfortable with how I behaved yesterday because I realized I might have offended you. Did you feel the same way?" The other person may think it was no big deal.

Be sincere. A sincere apology requires three steps. First, don't blame what happened on other people or circumstances. Second, acknowledge how your actions affected the other person – which means listening without defending yourself. Third, explain what you will do differently in the future to avoid making the same mistake. Such an apology might sound like, "I want to apologize for what I said yesterday. After speaking with you, I can hear how much my comments offended you and caused embarrassment. I want you to know that in the future I will be more sensitive."

Humor works. A little self-deprecating humor can save you, but make sure it is really only directed at yourself and does not increase anybody else's level of discomfort. Sometimes humor breaks the tension and provides an opening for you to recover.

Monitor future behavior. Communication has a cumulative effect. Every impression you make builds on the previous one. Overcoming a bad impression requires that all future behavior be consistent with how you want to be perceived. It will take time and trust to change perceptions, but it can be done!

Source: **"Overcoming a Bad First Impression," by Susan Fee, www.susanfee.com**

B Pair work Read the article again. Then take turns summarizing the advice in your own words.

C Group work Discuss these questions. Then share your answers with the class.

1. How effective do you think the advice in the article would be in changing a bad first impression?
2. How could an incident get blown out of proportion if someone doesn't apologize right away?
3. Do you believe that time and trust can change a negative perception? Explain.

3 SCIENCE AND TECHNOLOGY

LESSON A ▶ *Good science, bad science*

1 STARTING POINT
What's new?

A Read about these advances in science. What are the possible benefits and dangers?

DNA for Information Storage
Incredibly, scientists can now synthesize DNA to hold digital information, such as a video or text. The information can later be read by machines called DNA sequencers. DNA offers the longest duration for digital storage, keeping data safe for tens of thousands of years.

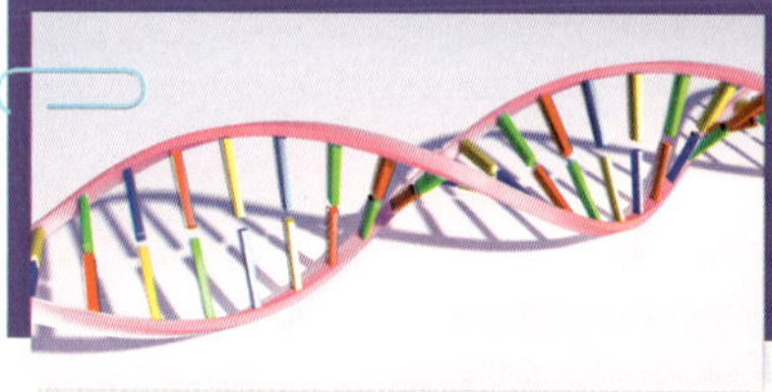

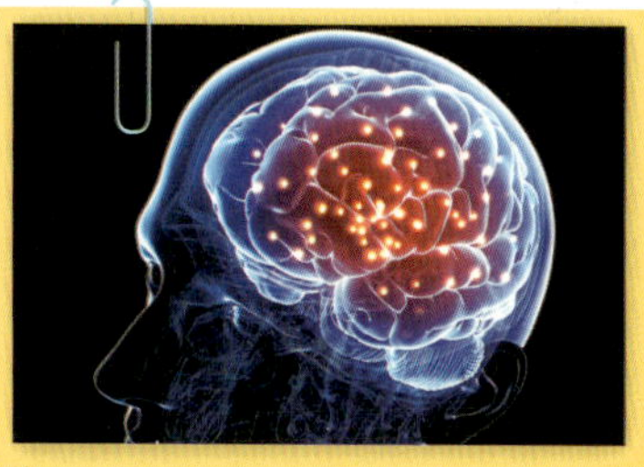

Thought Identification
Technology can already identify thoughts from scans of activity patterns in the human brain. The first attempts identified simple thoughts, but researchers are finding ways to reveal more complex thoughts and intentions.

Animal Cloning
With just one cell from a live or dead animal, an exact copy of the animal can be created with a technique known as cloning. The technique has been used to clone various pets, and cloned horses can even take part in the Olympics now.

B Pair work Read more about the scientific advances in part A. Do you think each statement is a good idea (*G*) or a bad idea (*B*)? Discuss each statement with a partner.

____ 1. DNA storage could one day provide so much storage space that no data would ever need to be erased again.

____ 2. Instead of questionnaires, marketers have used brain scans to check customer responses to products.

____ 3. Scientists have successfully stored a song in the DNA of living bacteria.

____ 4. An application of thought-identification technology allows a person to type on a computer just by thinking.

____ 5. To avoid taking any more animals from the wild, some scientists hope to clone endangered animals for use in zoos.

____ 6. Scientists want to create a clone from the frozen remains of an extinct mammoth.

2 LISTENING & SPEAKING
The effects of technology

A Listen to a show about driverless car technology. Choose the areas in which the impact of the technology would be mostly positive according to the speakers.

☐ accidents ☐ fuel consumption ☐ car repair
☐ road construction ☐ parking ☐ traffic

B Listen again and take notes about the impact of driverless car technology on the areas in part A. Then take turns describing the impact with a partner.

C Pair work Give an example of a new technology that has reshaped your daily life. What are the positive effects? What are the negative consequences?

3 GRAMMAR

Indefinite and definite articles

Review these rules for the indefinite articles *a* and *an* and the definite article *the*.

Use an indefinite article (*a* or *an*) when you mention a singular countable noun for the first time, or no article for plural countable and uncountable nouns. When you refer to the same item again, use *the*.
With just one cell from **a** live or dead **animal**, an exact copy of **the animal** can be created.

If you use a plural noun to make a general statement, do not use an article. However, if you make the same statement using a singular noun, use *the* or *a* / *an*.
Technology can already identify thoughts from scans of activity patterns in **human brains**.
Technology can already identify thoughts from scans of activity patterns in **the / a human brain**.

When making a general statement, do not use an article with uncountable nouns (*technology*, *education*, *shopping*, *love*, etc.).
DNA offers the longest duration for digital **storage**.

Use *the* with superlatives and with sequence markers such as *first*, *last*, *next*, etc., but don't use *the* with time expressions such as *last night* or *next month*.
The first attempts identified simple thoughts.

GRAMMAR PLUS *see page 110*

A Look at the Starting Point on page 18 again. Can you find other examples of article usage for each rule in the grammar box?

B Complete these sentences with the correct article. Write *X* where none is needed.

1. Nowadays, _X_ tracking technologies enable ____ websites to trace what online shoppers buy.
2. In some countries, ____ brain-scan evidence has been used in court to help convict killers.
3. ____ robot at Stanford University has used tools to successfully assemble ____ bookcase.
4. ____ first microbes able to consume oil were created to help clean up ____ oil spills.
5. Cloning could bring ____ animal back from extinction provided that DNA of ____ animal is still available.
6. I'm sure that a new computer will be even less expensive ____ next year.
7. It's a fact that ____ wireless technology makes the Internet available on a much wider scale.
8. For me, ____ most interesting new transportation technology is ____ driverless car.

C Pair work Write statements about the items below. Then discuss your ideas with a partner.

1. the most interesting electronic device in stores
2. the most exciting app or software on the market
3. the greatest advance in medicine
4. the most amazing invention of the twentieth century

"For me, the most interesting electronic device is the personal 3-D viewer."
"Oh, yeah. I tried one in a store. It feels just like you're in a movie theater."

4 VOCABULARY
A brave new world

A Match the words on the left with their definitions on the right.

1. audacious ____	a. silly and wasteful; carelessly self-indulgent
2. confidential ____	b. avoiding unnecessary risks
3. frivolous ____	c. having a willingness to take risks
4. hazardous ____	d. private or secret
5. problematic ____	e. against accepted beliefs about good behavior
6. prudent ____	f. dangerous
7. unethical ____	g. full of difficulties that are hard to solve

B Complete the sentences with the words in part A. Then compare your answers with a partner. Sometimes more than one answer is possible.

1. Sadly, much of our ____________ personal information is now on the Internet.
2. While switching to driverless cars would have benefits, the possible disruption to the economy makes the switch ____________.
3. Some ____________ scientists think it would be wise to do more research before using genetically modified plants in food.
4. Some people feel that denying any patient access to medical technology due to cost is ____________.
5. Due to its potential for serious accidents, many believe nuclear power is too ____________ to use safely.
6. One bold and ____________ dream of thought-identification researchers is to create a machine that can read all human thought.
7. With thousands of dogs and cats looking for homes, cloning additional ones for pets seems ____________.

VOCABULARY PLUS *see page 132*

5 DISCUSSION
Pros and cons

Group work Look at these news headlines. Discuss the positive effects and negative consequences of the events in the headlines.

Cosmetic Surgery Better and Cheaper Than Ever

Many men and women today are considering

Use of Personal Data by Social Media Sites Raises Privacy Concerns

Concerns rise as more social media sites use

More Farmers Plant Genetically Engineered Crops to Save Money

Microchip Implant Allows Criminals to Be Followed 24 Hours a Day

There is a debate over whether or not microchip

"Too many people are having cosmetic surgery for frivolous reasons these days. They should think twice about all the potential risks."

"Well, I'm all for it as long as people are prudent."

Useful expressions

Expressing caution and confidence

I'm a bit leery of . . .
You should think twice about . . .
I'm all for . . .
I have every confidence that . . .

6 WRITING

Writing summaries

When you write a summary, state in your own words the main points of a text, leaving out most of the supporting details. The summary must accurately reflect the ideas of the original text.

A Read the article and underline the main points.

ANIMAL CLONING
BENEFITS AND CONCERNS

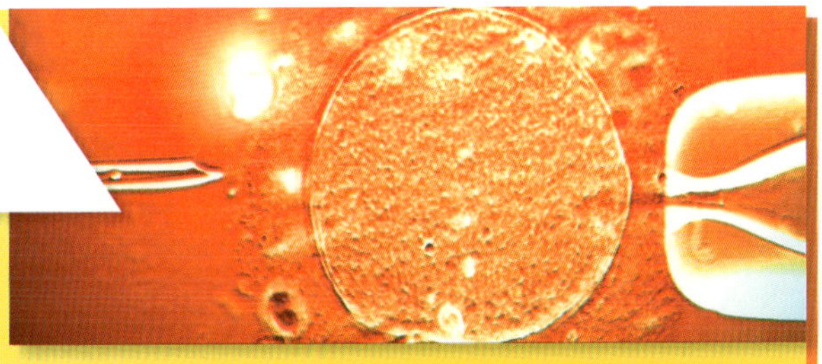

Animal cloning is the technique of creating an exact genetic copy of an animal from a single cell. It has previously been used to create copies of, for example, sheep, cows, and cats. While animal cloning is an amazing and powerful technology with possible benefits to science and humanity, many people are voicing concerns about the ethics and wisdom of this scientific innovation.

On the surface, animal cloning simply seems to be the "copying" of an animal, and it is difficult to see the benefits. However, the potential benefits of animal cloning are many. Cloned animals can be useful in the production of certain drugs to treat human illnesses. Through cloning, scientists can modify animal organs, such as heart valves, so that they can be safely transplanted into the human body. Cloning could also be very useful in saving endangered species. Two types of Asian cattle, the gaur and the banteng, have been helped in this way. Furthermore, cloning can be used to produce animals that are unable to reproduce naturally, such as mules.

Those who argue against cloning warn of its dangers. Organs transplanted from animals to humans might not always be safe, and there is a risk of disease. Additionally, for every animal that is successfully cloned, there are frequently a number of others that are not healthy enough to live. Cloned animals can also be weaker than those born by normal reproduction. When it comes to saving endangered animals, critics argue that cloning is too expensive and takes the attention and resources away from the real problem – the destruction of animal habitat.

In conclusion, it is unlikely that people on the two sides of the animal cloning issue will arrive at an agreement any time soon. But, as scientific progress presents us with new technologies such as animal cloning, it is important to discuss their benefits and voice our concerns about their use.

B Read the summary. Some main points from the article are not included. What are they?

Summary

Animal cloning is a technique for creating a copy of an animal from a single cell. People who support animal cloning argue that it can be useful in the production of drugs and transplant organs for humans. They also point out its value in preserving endangered species. Those who are against animal cloning argue that its medical uses are actually unsafe, that it produces unhealthy animals, and that it distracts us from the real problems that endangered animals face.

C **Pair work** Find an article on technology or a related topic. Then choose an important paragraph, and write the main idea. Compare with your partner.

D Write a summary of all or part of the article in one or more paragraphs.

1 STARTING POINT
Technology troubles

A Read about three people who had trouble with technology. How would you have felt in their situation? What would you have done?

Stan, 36

"Working from home one Friday, I opened my company network login page. Unfortunately, I'd forgotten the password my boss had given me, and he had taken the day off. Being too embarrassed to call him at home, I had to go to work after all to access the network."

Peter, 18

"I had dinner plans with my parents, but I was still out hiking when I was supposed to meet them at the restaurant. I kept trying to call them, but the calls were dropped before I could even say hello. Having gotten several calls from me, my parents became really worried. They were relieved when I finally got through an hour later."

Vera, 24

"I had a great presentation ready for the business class I'm taking. Being a perfectionist, I had prepared it in detail on my laptop. The next day in class, my laptop crashed opening the file. Trying to stay calm, I gave the presentation as best I could from memory."

B Pair work What technology gives you the most trouble? Tell your partner a story of a time you had trouble with technology.

"Sometimes my Wi-Fi stops working. It's really frustrating. I remember one day . . ."

2 LISTENING
The convenience of technology?

A Listen to a comedian talk about problems he had with technology. Write the types of technology and the problems he mentions in the chart.

	Technology	Problem	Example
1.			
2.			
3.			

B Listen again. What examples does he give of how the problems affected him? Complete the chart.

C Pair work Have you had similar problems with technology? How could the comedian have avoided them?

3 GRAMMAR

-ing clauses

To express two actions performed by the same person or thing in a single sentence, we can include an *-ing* clause. An *-ing* clause contains an *-ing* participle.

The two actions happen at the same time or one action happens during another action.

The next day in class, my laptop crashed **opening** the file.
(My laptop crashed while / when it was opening the file.)

Trying to stay calm, I gave the presentation as best I could from memory.
(I was trying to stay calm while I gave the presentation.)

She is at her desk **typing** a paper.
(She is at her desk, and she is typing a paper.)

When one action happens before another action, use *having* + past participle.

Having gotten several calls from me, my parents became really worried.
(My parents got several calls from me, and then they became really worried.)

Reasons and explanations for actions can also be expressed with *-ing* clauses.

Being too embarrassed to call him at home, I had to go to work after all to access the network.
(Because I was too embarrassed to call him at home, I had to go to work.)

GRAMMAR PLUS *see page 111*

A Look at the Starting Point on page 22 again. Can you find more examples of *-ing* clauses in the stories?

B Combine the sentences using an *-ing* clause. Then compare answers with a partner.

1. I was unable to remember my password. I clicked the link to have it sent to my email.
   Being unable to remember my password, I clicked the link to have it sent to my email.
2. My computer froze up. It was streaming a movie I'd already paid for.
3. I am very clumsy. I tripped and broke my brand-new tablet.
4. Zoe smiled from ear to ear. Zoe took a picture of herself to post on her website.
5. Harry invited some friends to join a club. Harry used a social networking site to do this.
6. The police implanted the criminal with a microchip. The police easily tracked him to his hideout.
7. Wen learned a lot about cloud computing. Wen was reading *TechToday* magazine.
8. Mari just got her first smartphone. Mari now spends all of her extra money on apps.

C Pair work Complete the sentences with your own ideas. Compare answers with a partner.

1. Having broken my . . .
   cell phone, I finally had a good reason to upgrade to a better one.
2. Being a creative person, . . .
3. Trying to keep up with new technologies, . . .
4. Having purchased a new . . .

4 VOCABULARY & SPEAKING
Different attitudes

A Look at these expressions. Which ones express a positive attitude, a negative attitude, or a neutral attitude? Write +, –, or ~.

____ 1. aware of
____ 2. curious about
____ 3. sick of
____ 4. fed up with
____ 5. familiar with
____ 6. suspicious of
____ 7. intimidated by
____ 8. knowledgeable about
____ 9. crazy about
____ 10. reliant on
____ 11. grateful for
____ 12. leery of

B **Group work** Look at the list of inventions and technologies. Can you think of more? What are your feelings about them? Discuss with your group.

1. spacecraft for private flights
2. touch-screen technology
3. speech-translation technology
4. video surveillance
5. wearable electronics
6. mobile apps
7. laser surgery
8. robots

"So, what do you think about spacecraft for private flights?"
"I'm a little intimidated by the idea of being in space. I'm curious about it, but I wouldn't try it."

VOCABULARY PLUS *see page 132*

5 DISCUSSION
Tech savvy?

A Are you a technophile or a technophobe? Complete the survey to find out.

TECHNOPHILE or TECHNOPHOBE?

	Agree (2 pts.)	Not Sure (1 pt.)	Disagree (0 pts.)
1. If technology permits it, I would favor the development of machines that surpass humans in intelligence.	☐	☐	☐
2. Governments need to generously fund research and development in technology.	☐	☐	☐
3. Everyone should try to stay informed about the latest innovations in technology.	☐	☐	☐
4. Genetic technologies should be used to gradually improve the human body over the course of generations.	☐	☐	☐
5. Science and technology will someday solve the world's problems of famine, war, disease, and overcrowding.	☐	☐	☐
6. It's important to acquire new technological devices shortly after they come out.	☐	☐	☐
7. Social media has a positive effect on people's social lives.	☐	☐	☐
8. Being connected to the Internet is a human right.	☐	☐	☐

SCORE

0–4 You are a technophobe, a person who has a strong mistrust of technology.

5–8 While not in love with technology, you see the need for it in our world.

9–12 You're a fan of technology and may be showing some signs of being a geek.

13–16 You're a technophile, a person who is crazy about technology.

B **Group work** Discuss your answers to the survey. Talk about the reasons for your choices and whether or not you agree with your score.

6 READING

A holiday from technology

A Pair work Scan the article. Which of the technologies mentioned do you use? How would your life change if you stopped using them for six months? Discuss with a partner. Then read the article.

I Took My Kids Offline

Susan Maushart was fed up. All she usually saw of her 15-year-old son, Bill, was the back of his head as he played video games. Her elder daughter, Anni, 18, had become overly reliant on social networking sites, and 14-year-old Sussy seemed physically attached to her laptop, often staying logged on to the Internet through the night.

"My concern," she says, "was that we had ceased to function as a family. We were just a collection of individuals who were very connected outwards – to friends, business, school, and sources of entertainment and information. But we simply weren't connecting with one another in real space and time in any sort of authentic way."

Having decided to take action, Maushart came up with a plan. She initiated an "experiment in living" and banned all technology at home for six months. Her kids really didn't believe her at first, but once they realized their mother was serious, they adapted well to an offline world.

Anni, Bill, and Sussy confronted boredom – something that they were previously unfamiliar with because of their endless access to online entertainment. They found out that it made them resourceful. Indeed, their mother thinks boredom is fundamentally important in terms of creativity: "If nothing's wrong, you're never motivated to change, to move out of that comfort zone."

Maushart had high expectations for her experiment: "I hoped that it would transform our lives – that we would become a closer family, read more, sit around the table to eat and play more music . . . that we would feel closer to one another." To her delight, many of these expectations were met.

During their half-year of technological deprivation, the family did eat together more regularly. They talked more. They played board games. They went on outings to the cinema and restaurants. Anni started studying in the university library. Bill rediscovered his saxophone and got into reading novels. Sussy, as the youngest and most technologically literate, struggled more, but eventually succumbed.

The family hasn't remained app-free, but there have been permanent changes. Because they'd come to understand how it was interfering with their social life, her older two teenagers have both taken holidays from Facebook. Bill sold his game console to buy a new saxophone, and Anni still prefers to study in the library, in a social-networking-free zone.

Maushart's children have all expressed a willingness to go offline again. It is something she too would love to do. "I'd look forward to a technology vacation," she says, "just like I look forward to going on a yoga retreat. I see it as an intermittent thing that straightens your head out, not a way of life."

Source: "Family: I Unplugged My Kids," by Melissa McClements, *The Guardian*

B Group work Discuss these questions. Then share your answers with the class.

1. What effects did Maushart's experiment have on her family? Was it a success?
2. How did being bored increase Anni, Bill, and Sussy's resourcefulness? Would it increase yours?
3. Would taking a "holiday from technology" be beneficial to most people? Why or why not?

COMMUNICATION REVIEW
UNITS 1–3

SELF-ASSESSMENT

How well can you do these things? Choose the best answer.

I can . . .	Very well	OK	A little
▸ Understand a conversation about people's appearance and personality (Ex. 1)	☐	☐	☐
▸ Take part in a discussion about attitudes toward clothes and fashion (Ex. 2)	☐	☐	☐
▸ Take part in a discussion about the impact of technology on people's lives (Ex. 3)	☐	☐	☐
▸ Take part in a discussion about issues associated with technology (Ex. 4)	☐	☐	☐

Now do the corresponding exercises. Was your assessment correct?

1 LISTENING
Class reunion

A Listen to a conversation between two friends. What is Karla trying to do? Choose the correct answer.

☐ a. She's trying to set up her personal profile on a social networking site.
☐ b. She's using a website to organize a class reunion.
☐ c. She's replying to messages she got from ex-classmates.

B Listen again. Are these statements true or false? Choose the correct answer.

	True	False
1. Karla is intimidated by the website technology.	☐	☐
2. Lucy isn't sure that the reunion will be completely harmonious.	☐	☐
3. Neither woman liked Andrew very much.	☐	☐
4. Renée's fashion taste has changed since she was in high school.	☐	☐
5. Mike's style has changed since he was in high school.	☐	☐

2 SPEAKING
Fashion statements

A Which of these statements about clothing do you agree with most?

- What you wear is who you are.
- People often discriminate against others because of the way they dress.
- Buying new clothes all the time is unethical.
- Clothes are like art that you wear.
- People who are interested in fashion are shallow and superficial.

B **Group work** Compare and explain your answers to part A. Try to find two statements that you all agree with.

3 DISCUSSION
Technological advances

A Which of these advances in technology has had the most positive or negative impact on our lives?

social media

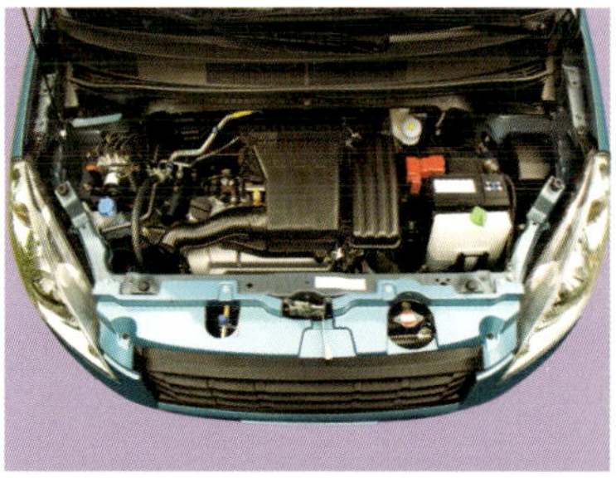

internal combustion engine

genetically modified food

large-scale farming

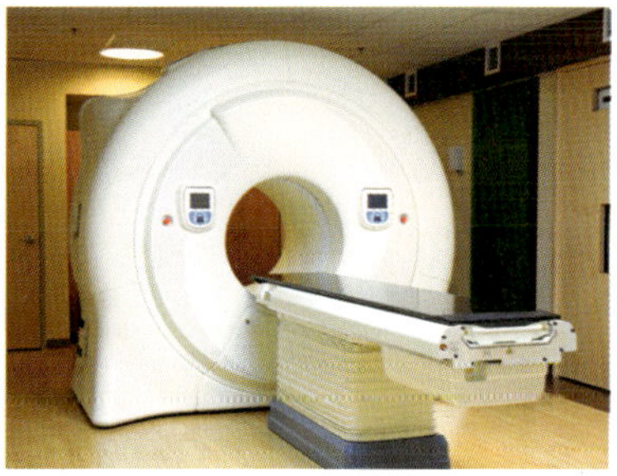

medical technology

renewable energy technology

B Pair work Compare your answers with a partner.

"I think social media has had the most positive impact on our lives. We are so much more connected than we were a few years ago."

"Well, that's true, but medical technology has had more of a positive influence on people around the world."

4 DISCUSSION
Is technology good or bad?

A Read these opinions about technology. What are the main issues they raise? What's your own point of view on these issues?

When you are ready to invest in a new technology, there are a few questions you should ask yourself. First, is the new item cheaper than what it replaces? Does it save space? Will it make your life easier? Is it energy efficient? Will you be able to recycle it or at least dispose of it properly? If not, don't buy it.

— Kwang-hyun Lee, Busan, Korea

How we think about technology is flawed. We are overeager to have the newest gadget. We are too impressed by speed, noise, compactness, and general flashiness. We need a more mature and cautious way of thinking about technology. New is not always better.

— Inés Candia, Asunción, Paraguay

B Group work Compare your ideas. Are your points of view similar? How?

4 SUPERSTITIONS AND BELIEFS

LESSON A ▶ *Superstitions*

1 STARTING POINT

The things people believe!

A Read the list of superstitions. Do you believe in any of them?

Beliefs Across Cultures

In Turkey, many people agree that when someone goes on a journey, you should pour water on the ground behind him or her to bring the person back safely.

In Brazil, people claim you should enter a place using your right foot to have good fortune.

In Russia, looking into a broken mirror will bring bad luck.

In Italy, many people believe that if visitors toss a coin into the Trevi Fountain in Rome, they will return to that city in the future.

In Japan, it is very bad luck to give a present that consists of four pieces.

In Venezuela, some people say that if someone passes a broom over your feet, you will never get married.

In Greece, you should place your shoes with the soles on the floor when you take them off because overturned shoes are considered unlucky.

B Pair work Which superstitions do some people in your culture believe?

2 VOCABULARY

Expressions with *luck*

A Match the statements with the replies containing *luck*.

1. "I've got to go. I have a big test tomorrow." ____
2. "I'm out of cash. Is there an ATM nearby?" ____
3. "He won the first game of chess he ever played!" ____
4. "He lost his job and house, and now he's sick." ____
5. "Are you going to Europe this summer?" ____
6. "How did you win those soccer tickets?" ____
7. "Thanks for the $20. Can I have $40 more?" ____

a. "That was beginner's luck."
b. "No such luck. I'm staying home."
c. "I'm afraid you're out of luck."
d. "Wow! He's got bad luck."
e. "Well, best of luck!"
f. "Don't push your luck."
g. "It was the luck of the draw."

B Pair work Use the expressions with *luck* to write short conversations. Act them out with your partner.

"I really want tickets to the Jay Z concert."
"I'm afraid you're out of luck. They sold out in 10 minutes!"

VOCABULARY PLUS *see page 133*

3 GRAMMAR

Reporting clauses

To report what someone says, thinks, believes, etc., you can use a sentence that includes a reporting clause. The use of the word *that* is optional.

In Turkey, **many people agree (that)** when someone goes on a journey, you should pour water on the ground behind him or her to bring the person back safely.

In Venezuela, **some people say (that)** if someone passes a broom over your feet, you will never get married.

The following verbs are often used in reporting clauses.

More formal: argue assert claim report

More conversational: admit agree assume believe doubt explain feel say

GRAMMAR PLUS *see page 112*

A Look at the Starting Point on page 28 again. Can you find two other sentences that contain reporting clauses? For the sentences that don't, add a reporting clause and rewrite the sentence.

B Rewrite each sentence with a reporting clause. Use a different reporting verb to introduce each one.

1. Everyone is superstitious about a few things.
   Many people agree that almost everyone is superstitious about a few things.
2. It's fine to follow superstitions for fun, but not to really believe in them.
3. Superstitions are an important part of our cultural heritage.
4. Superstitions are dangerous because they prevent people from thinking scientifically.
5. Many holiday rituals are based on ancient beliefs and superstitions.
6. Superstitions sometimes contain truths handed down from the past.

C Pair work Share your answers with your partner. Then give your opinions about the statements.

"Many people agree that almost everyone is superstitious about a few things. It's true! When I spill some salt, I always throw a little over my left shoulder so I don't have bad luck."

4 DISCUSSION

Everyday superstitions

A Pair work Do you know any superstitions connected with these things? Describe them to your partner.

- animals and plants
- days, dates, or months
- household objects
- clothing
- food
- colors
- money
- numbers
- weddings

B Group work Join another pair and compare your answers. Ask follow-up questions.

"In parts of Great Britain, people who aren't feeling well sometimes stick coins into the trunk of a tree that has fallen down."

"Why is that?"

"Well, some people believe that if you put a coin in wood, it can make illnesses go away. They call these trees 'wishing trees.'"

5 LISTENING

Common explanations

A Listen to people talk about superstitions. What superstitions are they talking about? How is each superstition explained?

B Listen again. Answer these questions.

1. How did the woman with allergies react to the man's explanation?
2. Why did the son feel it was necessary to say that he was only kidding?
3. Why does the man suggest not telling Mr. Wilson that being left-handed was once thought to be suspicious?

6 DISCUSSION

Are you superstitious?

A Pair work Take turns interviewing each other, and complete the questionnaire. Then calculate your scores.

Lucky or Unlucky?

	YES (1 pt.)	NO (0 pt.)
1. Is it unlucky not to say something like "Bless you!" when someone sneezes?	☐	☐
2. Are there any particular days that you consider unlucky?	☐	☐
3. Do you have any lucky numbers?	☐	☐
4. Do you think some colors bring good luck?	☐	☐
5. Do you avoid walking under a ladder because it might bring you bad luck?	☐	☐
6. Are there any animals you consider unlucky?	☐	☐
7. Do you believe that certain actions before a wedding bring good or bad luck?	☐	☐
8. Do you carry any good luck charms or have any in your house?	☐	☐
9. Do you have a piece of clothing that brings you good luck?	☐	☐
10. Do you avoid having specific items in your house because they might bring bad luck?	☐	☐

SCORE

0–1	Life is not a matter of luck to you!	**5–7**	You're fairly superstitious, aren't you?
2–4	You're not very superstitious, but . . .	**8–10**	Wow! You're really superstitious!

B Group work Compare your scores. Then explain some of the things you're superstitious about. Is there anything else that you think brings good or bad luck?

"Well, when I talk about something that's going well, I say 'knock on wood.'"
"Really? Why do you do that?"
"Well, they say that if you knock on something made of wood, your luck will continue."

7 WRITING
Restating a thesis

The first paragraph of a composition provides the thesis statement and sometimes gives general examples. The last paragraph restates the thesis statement.

A Read this composition. Find the thesis statement and a supporting example in the first paragraph. Then look at the last paragraph. Which sentence restates the thesis statement?

SUPERSTITIONS: HARD TO IGNORE

Some people think that certain objects bring them good luck; others avoid certain things or situations that they believe might bring them bad luck. Even people who claim not to believe in superstitions sometimes use phrases such as "knock on wood" when they speak. Superstitions concerning both good and bad luck are part of everyone's life in the United States – even if you don't believe in them, they are difficult to ignore.

It's easy to find superstitions relating to good luck. For example, my friend Irene carries a fake rabbit's foot in her pocket to bring her good luck. Another friend, who plays baseball, panics whenever his mother washes his "lucky" baseball socks. My mother believes that nine is her lucky number, and even my level-headed father has hung a horseshoe over the entrance of our home to bring us good luck and good fortune.

Superstitions concerning bad luck are just as common. My mother believes that certain days are bad for events like marriages and ceremonies, while my uncle always says "knock on wood" and then looks for something made of wood to knock on with his hand. Then there's my friend who goes out of his way to avoid black cats. My sister never puts her bag on the floor because she thinks doing so will bring her bad luck.

Personally, I am not very superstitious. I don't have any lucky socks, and I don't have any lucky or unlucky numbers. Still, I find myself avoiding black cats, and I knock on wood every now and then. Superstitions are just a part of life, whether you believe them or not.

B Write a composition about superstitions and good and bad luck in your culture. Do your first and last paragraphs follow the guidelines stated in the box above?

C Pair work Exchange your composition with a partner, and answer these questions.

1. Does the first paragraph contain a thesis statement and give general examples?
2. How well do the examples in the middle paragraphs support the thesis? Are there enough examples?
3. Does the last paragraph restate the thesis?

LESSON B ▶ *Believe it or not*

1 STARTING POINT
Fact or fiction?

A Three of these news stories are true and one is false. Decide which one is false.

1

A company has produced a device designed to chase away loitering children and teenagers. It was explained that the device emits a sound that irritates young people.

2

It's been confirmed that if an egg is placed directly between two cell phones that are in "talk mode," the egg will be cooked in about an hour.

3

A candy company is selling lollipops with a variety of insects inside, including crickets, ants, and scorpions. It is claimed that the lollipops are actually quite tasty.

4

It was reported that a website broadcast live video of a wheel of cheddar cheese as it ripened. It is said that the video ran for over nine months.

B **Pair work** Tell your partner your choice and explain why you think it is false. (For the answer, see page 142.)

2 VOCABULARY & SPEAKING
That sounds fishy!

A Which of these words describe something likely to be true? Which describe something likely to be fabricated? Divide them into two groups. Then add two more items to each group.

believable	convincing	dubious	fishy	misleading	plausible
conceivable	credible	far-fetched	iffy	phony	well-founded

B Use the words in part A to write about each story in the Starting Point.

The article about the candy company sounds completely phony to me. It's just not a plausible story.

C **Group work** Take turns making statements, some true and some false, about yourself to your group. Respond using the words describing truth and fabrication.

"I have a very good singing voice, and I sing with a band on the weekend."
"Well, your speaking voice is very nice, so that seems pretty believable to me."

VOCABULARY PLUS *see page 133*

3 GRAMMAR

Reporting clauses in the passive

To report a general claim or opinion, you can use a passive form of a reporting verb and *it*. Notice that the agent is often omitted and understood to be "some people" or "many people."

It was explained (that) the device emits a sound that irritates young people.

It is said (that) the video ran for over nine months.

GRAMMAR PLUS *see page 113*

A Look at the Starting Point on page 32 again. Can you find other examples of reporting clauses in the passive?

B Rewrite these statements with a reporting clause in the passive with *it*.

1. People estimate that 50 percent of the population believes in ghosts.
   It is estimated that 50 percent of the population believes in ghosts.
2. Some sources say that the idea of horseshoes being lucky dates back to the ancient Greeks.
3. Many claim that some people can communicate with plants.
4. People once thought the sun moved around the earth.
5. Some sources have reported that practical jokes on April 1 are becoming less common.
6. Experts argue that people create Internet hoaxes for a wide variety of reasons.
7. Sociologists think that people developed the first superstitions in an attempt to gain control over things they didn't understand.
8. People too easily assume that just because something is in print, it's true.

C Pair work Use reporting clauses in the passive to talk about these interesting facts.

1. A company makes a bicycle that seats seven people.
2. A 33-year-old man married a 104-year-old woman.
3. On April 1, 2006, a flight was denied permission to land because the air traffic controller was on a tea break.
4. Butterflies can taste with their feet.
5. You can send a coconut through the mail in the United States without any wrapping.
6. A crocodile measuring over six meters long was found in the Philippines.
7. The world's first webcam was used to let staff in a university computer department see the office coffee pot.

"Get this – it's been reported that a company makes a bicycle that seats seven people."

Useful expressions

Reporting something surprising

Get this – . . .
Believe it or not, . . .
Did you hear what happened?

D Pair work Complete these statements about beliefs using your own information. Compare your statements with a partner.

1. People don't believe this anymore, but it used to be said that . . .
2. Recently, it has been reported in the news that . . .

4 LISTENING
Shocking news

A Look at the map of Belgium. What do you know about this country?

B Listen to a conversation about a journalistic hoax that affected many people in Belgium. What was the hoax?

C Listen again. Which events actually happened? Choose the correct answers.

☐ 1. The king and queen left the country.
☐ 2. People panicked.
☐ 3. A television station website crashed.
☐ 4. Foreign ambassadors called the Belgian authorities.

5 DISCUSSION
Internet hoaxes

A Pair work Have you ever read or heard about something on the Internet that was a hoax? Tell your partner about it.

B Pair work Read these claims found on the Internet. Choose the ones you think are hoaxes. Then discuss with a partner. (For the answers, see page 142.)

Website Claims

	HOAX?
1. A man offers $10,000 to anyone who can find him a wife.	☐
2. There is a group dedicated to preventing cruelty to insects throughout the world.	☐
3. Each year, the Internet must be shut down for 24 hours to allow authorities to clean it.	☐
4. There is a new chewing gum that you can recharge with flavor when the taste fades.	☐
5. An 85-year-old woman is training to climb Mount Everest with her little dog.	☐
6. An adventure company is now reserving seats for a trip to the center of the earth.	☐
7. A new technology allows you to get a suntan from your computer screen.	☐
8. A company can deliver tacos to homes using delivery robots.	☐

C Group work Discuss these questions with your group.

1. Which of the website claims seems the most plausible to you? Which seems the most iffy? Why?
2. Why do you think people create hoax websites and hoax emails?
3. Do you think people who create Internet hoaxes should be punished?

6 READING
Athletes and their superstitions

A Pair work Research suggests that good luck charms and lucky rituals can actually have an effect on an athlete's performance. Why might this be so? Discuss with a partner. Then read the article.

DO GOOD LUCK CHARMS REALLY WORK IN COMPETITIONS?

To avoid jinxing herself, Canadian hurdler Angela Whyte never carries her podium clothes with her to the track at international competitions. But before the 100-meter hurdle final at the Commonwealth Games in New Delhi, Ms. Whyte faced a dilemma, because her roommate – whom she would usually ask to bring them – was gone for the day.

"I packed the podium clothes in a separate backpack, so they wouldn't touch the competition gear," she laughed, after winning a silver medal. "It's a little psycho, but it worked!"

Ms. Whyte isn't alone in her faith in the power of superstition. Numerous studies have examined the prevalence of "magical thinking" among athletes, finding that the greater the interest in sports, the more superstitious a person is likely to be.

Intrigued by stories about athletes such as Michael Jordan, who wore his old college shorts under his uniform throughout his professional career, Dr. Lysann Damisch led a study in which she found that following a lucky ritual enhances self-confidence. This leads one to set higher goals and be more persistent, ultimately achieving greater success.

Not all athletic rituals work this way, though. Dr. Damisch claims that routines such as bouncing a basketball exactly three times immediately before shooting a foul shot does more than simply boost confidence. This routine actually serves to focus attention and also triggers well-learned motor sequences. Other apparent superstitions may have more to do with creating a relaxed and positive mindset. Ms. Whyte, for example, always travels to competitions with a teddy bear named O.T. – but not because she believes O.T. brings her luck. "I've had him since I was two years old," she explains, "so he reminds me of my home and family when I'm traveling. He's my security blanket."

The effectiveness of superstitious rituals may explain why they have persisted across cultures and eras, Dr. Damisch points out. But there are limits to their power. Following such rituals "doesn't mean you win, because of course winning and losing is something else."

Source: "Do Good Luck Charms Really Work In Competitions?" by Alex Hutchinson, *The Globe and Mail*

B Read the article again. Are the statements true (*T*), false (*F*), or is the information not given (*NG*) in the article? Write the correct letters and correct the false statements.

____ 1. Angela Whyte considers her ritual of not carrying her podium clothes to the track completely rational.

____ 2. Those with an avid interest in sports are not likely to be influenced by superstitions.

____ 3. Dr. Damisch was fascinated by Michael Jordan's professional career.

____ 4. An increase in self-confidence can make people set and reach more challenging goals.

____ 5. Some lucky rituals actually help the brain and body prepare for performance.

C Group work Discuss these questions. Then share your answers with the class.

1. What other good luck charms and lucky rituals used in sports do you know about? How do they relate to the findings of the research mentioned in the text?
2. What things do you do to increase confidence and keep a positive mindset? Which is most effective?

5 MOVIES AND TELEVISION

LESSON A ▶ *Movies*

1 STARTING POINT

Movies today

A Read the statements about some movie trends. Which of these trends have you noticed?

Movie Trends

Unquestionably, studios are interested in producing a lot more movies about superheroes, because these are so popular with audiences! That's good news if you love superhero movies as much as I do! **—Maura B., Ireland**

For a long time, box office hits were predictably followed by sequels. But nowadays, the production of prequels has become a pretty exciting trend. **—Alejandro H., Mexico**

Box office profits will possibly continue to fall in the United States. Fortunately, for the movie studios, revenues continue to increase in several overseas markets. **—Naomi S., the United States**

Independent filmmakers often go into debt producing their movies, so many now turn to crowdsourcing websites for funding. Many fans like me make donations to film projects they support. **—Masako N., Japan**

Seemingly, there have been more women cast in leading roles in successful movies. Honestly, I hope that having more courageous heroines will be a trend that lasts and not just a passing fad. **—Leonard W., Canada**

Overall, the animated movies I take my children to see these days are visually spectacular and have sophisticated humor and storylines. Not surprisingly, the other adults I see at the theater also enjoy these movies as much as the kids do. **—Lucas M., Brazil**

B Pair work What other movie trends have you noticed? Discuss them with your partner.

"It seems to me that quite a few plays and musicals are being made into movies lately."

2 VOCABULARY

Reacting to movies

A Do these adjectives have a positive or a negative meaning? Mark them + or –.

____ a. clichéd	____ d. inspiring	____ g. predictable
____ b. engrossing	____ e. mediocre	____ h. riveting
____ c. formulaic	____ f. moving	____ i. touching

B Complete the sentences with the adjectives from part A. Sometimes more than one answer is possible.

1. ________________ movies affect your emotions or bring tears to your eyes.
2. A/An ________________ movie completely captures your attention.
3. A/An ________________ movie isn't very good, and probably not worth watching.
4. A movie is ________________ if its plot is obvious and you can guess the ending.

VOCABULARY PLUS *see page 134*

3 GRAMMAR

Sentence adverbs

Sentence adverbs modify a whole sentence, not just part of it. Many adverbs can be used in this way. Sentence adverbs express the speaker's attitude, opinion, or reason for speaking.

Certainty: *clearly, definitely, obviously, unquestionably*
Unquestionably, studios are interested in producing a lot more movies about superheroes.

Less certainty: *apparently, seemingly, supposedly*
Seemingly, there have been more women cast in leading roles in successful movies.

Possibility and probability: *possibly, potentially, probably*
Box office profits will **possibly** continue to fall in the United States.

Talking honestly and directly: *frankly, honestly, seriously*
Honestly, I hope that having more courageous heroines will be a trend that lasts and not just a passing fad.

Summarizing: *basically, essentially, fundamentally, mainly, overall*
Overall, the animated movies I take my children to see these days are visually spectacular.

Other attitudes: *amazingly, surprisingly, not surprisingly, predictably, fortunately, unfortunately*
Not surprisingly, the other adults I see at the theater also enjoy these movies as much as the kids do.

GRAMMAR PLUS *see page 114*

A Look at the Starting Point on page 36 again. Can you find other sentences with adverbs from the grammar box? What attitude or opinion do they convey?

B Pair work Rewrite each sentence using one of the adverbs from the grammar box. Compare with a partner.

1. No one is surprised that movie attendance is declining in the United States due to the many forms of home entertainment available.
   Not surprisingly, movie attendance is declining in the United States due to the many forms of home entertainment available.
2. It's been said that men prefer action movies while women favor romantic ones.
3. It's likely that more and more independent films will win awards in the future.
4. In truth, many people enjoy engrossing movies full of action and special effects.
5. It's clear that in the future nearly all movies will be shot and projected using digital technology instead of film.
6. A potential result is that young filmmakers may never use film.
7. It's amazing that studios routinely spend hundreds of millions of dollars to make a movie.
8. It's possible that watching violent movies can make some children more aggressive.

C Group work Use sentence adverbs to express your attitude about trends in the areas below, or use your own ideas. Listen to your classmates' reactions.

- shopping
- television
- music
- smartphones
- transportation
- computers
- magazines
- video games
- language learning

"You can supposedly get discounts from stores by indicating you like them on social media sites."

"Really? I'll have to give that a try. Frankly, I hate paying full price for anything."

4 LISTENING
Behind all good movies . . .

A **Pair work** Look at the movie genres. What elements do you consider essential for each genre? Discuss with a partner.

animated movies   musicals   romantic comedies   sci-fi movies

B Listen to four people talk about key elements of the movie genres in part A. Complete the chart with the genre each speaker is talking about.

	Movie genre	Key elements
1. Heather		
2. Josh		
3. Felipe		
4. Dana		

C Listen again. What three elements does each person consider essential for each movie genre? Complete the chart. Are their opinions similar to yours?

5 DISCUSSION
Movie genre preferences

A **Pair work** Discuss the results of this survey on movie genre preferences. Do you think the preferences are the same where you live?

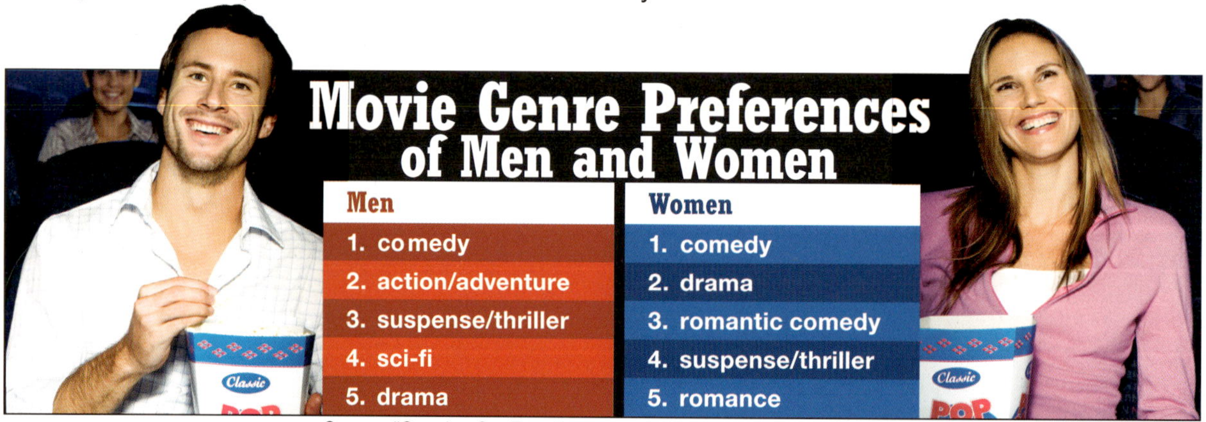

Source: "Opening Our Eyes," a study by Northern Alliance and Ipsos MediaCT for the British Film Institute

B **Group work** Discuss different aspects of each movie genre in the survey. What is it about them that men, women, or both might like?

"Thriller movies often have riveting action scenes. I think that's more of a guy thing."

"I don't agree. I think both genders enjoy thriller movies because of the element of surprise that many of them have."

C **Group work** Name actors and actresses who have starred in the various movie genres. Discuss their performances and whether the genre suits them.

"I think Will Smith is perfect in sci-fi movies. He can be serious and funny, which makes the movies riveting and entertaining."

"That's true. But I think he's better suited for comedies – when he's not serious at all!"

6 WRITING
Writing a movie review

An effective movie review generally provides information about the movie, summarizes the plot, and offers a recommendation based on the writer's opinion.

A Read the questions and the movie review. Underline the answers to the questions in the review and write the number of the question.

1. What is the title of the movie, and what genre is it?
2. What made you decide to watch the movie? What is your general impression?
3. What is the movie about?
4. Who are the main characters and actors? Who is the director?
5. Would you recommend this movie to others? Why or why not?

MOVIE REVIEW:
Safety Not Guaranteed

I'm a huge fan of both indie films and movies about time travel, so choosing to watch *Safety Not Guaranteed* was an easy decision to make and a very good one. *Safety Not Guaranteed* is an offbeat
1 romantic comedy with an original storyline, an excellent cast, and an unexpected ending. It's about time travel, but it's also about why people long to revisit the past and about why some people are willing to believe in the impossible.

Three magazine reporters from Seattle head out on an assignment to interview a guy who placed a classified ad looking for a partner to travel back in time with him. They think it's a joke, but as the movie progresses, they gradually discover that Kenneth (played by Mark Duplass), the would-be time-traveler, actually believes he's built a working time machine. Along the way, Darius (Aubrey Plaza), one of the reporters, falls in love with Kenneth. Meanwhile, Jeff (Jake Johnson), another one of the reporters, does some time-traveling of his own as he takes time off to look up an old girlfriend and teach Arnou (Karan Soni), the third reporter, a little bit about love. In the end, it all comes together in a marvelous way.

Directed by Colin Trevorrow, the movie is charming, likable, and funny. Every line of its clever script either makes you laugh or moves the story in a new direction. Best of all, it's a movie so magical that it might make you want to believe in time travel yourself. Highly recommended.

B Think of a movie you've seen recently, and make notes to answer the questions in part A. Then use your notes to write a movie review.

C Pair work Exchange your movie review with a partner, and answer these questions.

1. Does your partner's review answer all of the questions in part A? Find the answers.
2. Is the information in the review organized effectively? How could it be improved?
3. What else would you like to know about the movie reviewed? Ask at least two questions.
4. Would you follow the recommendation in your partner's review after reading it? Why or why not?

Useful expressions

Suggesting improvements

It might be better if you . . .
I think what it needs is . . .
You might want to . . .
It'd be even better if . . .

LESSON B ▶ *Television*

1 STARTING POINT
TV time

A Read these posts about TV programs. Which program would you most like to watch? Which one would least interest you? Why?

What's On? A Blog for TV Lovers

Today's Question: What TV shows could you watch over and over again?

Posted at 9:24 by Donna
House is such a riveting show that I could watch it again and again. Frankly, Dr. Gregory House (played by Hugh Laurie) is so foul-tempered that I hated him when I first started watching the show. But the amazing plots combining medical mysteries and detective work really drew me in. It's such a great show that I bought all eight seasons and have watched many episodes more than once.

Posted at 9:03 by Justin
I could watch many sitcoms forever, but my busy schedule leaves me so little TV time that I don't want to waste it watching mediocre sitcoms. So, I watch only the best ones, like *The Big Bang Theory*. It centers on the hilarious lives of four geeky scientists. The show's intelligent, witty dialogue is packed with so many great jokes that it's nonstop laughs from beginning to end.

Posted at 8:46 by Franco
I never get tired of watching *CSI*. The unique murder investigations are always thrilling! They include so many scientific details that I always learn something. Plus, I love the humor, and the chemistry between the characters is great! Some of my favorite actors are on *CSI New York*, so those are the episodes I stream the most.

B Pair work What are your favorite TV shows of all time? Why do you like them?

"One of my favorite shows is Law and Order, *a crime drama series. The plots are always engrossing with lots of surprising twists."*

2 VOCABULARY
Types of TV programs

A Pair work Look at the different types of TV programs. Select the ones that you know. Then ask a partner about the ones you don't know.

- ☐ 1. game show
- ☐ 2. soap opera
- ☐ 3. sitcom
- ☐ 4. cartoon
- ☐ 5. documentary
- ☐ 6. drama series
- ☐ 7. sports program
- ☐ 8. talk show
- ☐ 9. sketch comedy show
- ☐ 10. cooking show
- ☐ 11. reality TV show
- ☐ 12. news program

B Group work Which types of TV shows do you watch? Give an example of each.

VOCABULARY PLUS *see page 134*

3 GRAMMAR

Such . . . that and *so . . . that*

So **and** ***such, such . . . that, so . . . that, so much / little . . . that,*** **and** ***so many / few . . . that*** **are commonly used to express extremes in exclamatory sentences.**

a. ***Such*** **is followed by a noun (usually modified by an adjective).**
It's **such** a great show **that** I bought all eight seasons.

b. ***So*** **is followed by an adjective or adverb.**
Dr. House is **so** foul-tempered **that** I hated him when I first started watching the show.

c. ***So many*** **and** ***so few*** **are followed by countable nouns.**
The dialogue is packed with **so many** jokes **that** it's nonstop laughs from beginning to end.

d. ***So much*** **and** ***so little*** **are followed by uncountable nouns.**
My busy schedule leaves me **so little** TV time **that** I don't want to waste it watching mediocre sitcoms.

GRAMMAR PLUS *see page 115*

A Look at the Starting Point on page 40 again. Can you find more sentences with *so* and *such*? Which patterns do the sentences follow?

B Complete these sentences with *so many*, *so few*, *so much*, or *so little*.

1. My brother watches ___*so much*___ reality TV that he hardly does anything else.
2. There are ________________ fans of that drama series that it's consistently the highest rated show on TV.
3. There was ________________ interest in the cartoon that the network canceled it.
4. Bob knows ________________ useless facts that he should go on a trivia game show.
5. Ads for that new talk show generated ________________ hype that most viewers were disappointed once it came out.
6. There are ________________ trustworthy news programs that I've started going to reliable websites instead.

C Rewrite these sentences using *such . . . that* or *so . . . that*. Then compare with a partner.

1. The referee did a terrible job during the soccer game. My father was yelling at the TV set.
The referee did such a terrible job during the soccer game that my father was yelling at the TV set.
2. There are many TV programs available on the Internet. I'm using my TV set less and less.
3. That new sitcom was well reviewed. I wouldn't be surprised if it won an award.
4. Certain singers attract huge audiences. They charge ridiculously high prices for concert tickets.
5. Some documentaries today deal with critical social issues. They can have a political effect.

4 LISTENING
New TV shows

A Listen to some TV network employees discuss ideas for new shows with their boss, Rick. Write the type and the basic idea of each show in the chart.

	Café People	*Serve Yourself!*	*New Borders*
Type of show			
Basic idea			
Accepted?			
Reasons			

B Listen again. Were the show ideas accepted? Write *Yes* or *No* and Rick's reasons for the decisions in the chart.

C **Pair work** Make a list of three TV shows that are popular in your community. Then discuss the reasons why these programs are so popular.

"Modern Family *is a really popular comedy show. I think that's because it lets people laugh at problems all families have, and it's presented in an interesting fake documentary style."*

5 DISCUSSION
Your own TV show

A **Pair work** Work with your partner to develop a new TV show. Choose one of the genres in the form below or add one. Brainstorm ideas for the show. Then complete the form with your best ideas.

New TV Show Proposal Form

Title: ____________________

Genre: ☐ drama series ☐ game show ☐ reality TV show ☐ Other: ____________
☐ cooking show ☐ soap opera ☐ sitcom

Target audience (age, gender, etc.):

Basic idea of the show:

Casting ideas (Who will be on the show?):

Reasons people will want to watch it:

B **Group work** Role-play a meeting at a TV network. Present your show idea to the group and try to convince them to produce it. Then decide whose idea was the best.

6 READING
A movie starring everyone

A Pair work How could someone make a movie showing what life is like on a single day in every country on earth? What would a project like that involve? Discuss with a partner. Then read the article.

One Day on Earth:
A Time Capsule of Our Lives

It is considered one of the most audacious documentary film projects ever made: a film shot in every country of the world on the same day, involving 3,000 hours of footage in 70 languages from 19,000 volunteer filmmakers around the world. The 104-minute film, *One Day on Earth*, is a visual poem starring everyone on the planet. It's about you and me, the times we live in, and our place in the puzzle of humanity.

Director Kyle Ruddick and executive producer Brandon Litman are the two young forces behind *One Day on Earth*. They met at the University of Southern California, where Ruddick studied film and Litman majored in business. Although both had worked on short-length commercial and broadcast projects, they had never attempted anything like *One Day on Earth* – their first feature-length film – and neither had anyone else.

Ruddick and Litman came up with the idea for the film in 2008 at a world music festival, where they heard musicians who had never met before play together for the first time. After a few awkward attempts, the musicians soon discovered a way to create a beautiful fusion of music. In a similar way, "the editorial process was a process of discovery," said Ruddick. "You couldn't make this sort of film without being completely open to what you receive."

Common themes arose organically, and the filmmakers structured the documentary around film clips that underscore larger global issues. A sense of communal experience further grounded the wide-ranging film as the grassroots filmmakers worked to painstakingly capture the beauty and tragedy of the human experience.

In one of the more touching moments of *One Day on Earth*, a man looks into the camera and says, "I want to thank you for recording this story of my life and replaying it for others." He says he hopes the viewer may find a lesson in it. His words tap into greater truths about this time-capsule art – about how the drive to understand others often derives from a more personal need to understand ourselves.

The film is also about a need to reaffirm just how alike we are despite our outward differences. "The world is a vast spectacle that we indulge and love and also struggle through," said Ruddick. "We're born, we're young, we dance, we sing, and despite all of that, we have incredible challenges." Yet, "cinema is this universal language that anyone can understand and relate to," Ruddick said. "It goes beyond borders."

Source: "'One Day on Earth' Debuts Worldwide, Offers Time Capsule of Our Lives," by Mark Johanson, *International Business Times*

B Group work Discuss these questions. Then share your answers with the class.

1. What factors do you think had to come together to make *One Day on Earth* possible?
2. Do you agree with Ruddick that film is a universally understood language? Why or why not?
3. In your opinion, is it true that people all over the world are alike despite our outward differences? Explain.

6 MUSICIANS AND MUSIC

LESSON A ► *A world of music*

1 STARTING POINT
Taste in music

A Read the statements expressing different views on music. Which ones do you agree with?

Overheard on the Streets

1 "I think the more you like to dance, the more you appreciate music with a Latin beat."

2 "At first, I didn't like rap music. But the more I listened to the lyrics, the more I understood its powerful social message."

3 "Some of the greatest music is in movie soundtracks. The more exciting the soundtrack, the better the movie seems."

4 "Radio stations kill music sales by overplaying songs. The more I hear a pop song on the radio, the less I feel like buying it."

5 "I'm interested in how a band plays, not how it looks. The more a band focuses on its appearance, the less interesting the music is."

6 "Classical music has many layers of complexity. The more knowledgeable you are about it, the more you'll be able to enjoy it."

7 "TV commercials often feature a catchy tune – and the catchier the tune, the more likely you are to remember the name of the product."

8 "A lot of my friends like to go to clubs with really loud music, but not me. The louder the music gets, the sooner I feel like leaving."

B Pair work What kinds of things do you look for in new songs or artists? What makes certain songs more successful than others?

"I love sampling. You know, when artists mix older songs with new music and lyrics."

"Me, too. I like recognizable tunes, but with a new twist."

Useful expressions

Asking about opinions

What do you think of/about . . . ?
How do you feel about . . . ?
Are you into . . . ?

2 LISTENING
Awesome tunes

A Listen to Adam and Lisa talk about music. What are they doing?

B Listen again. What are the three types of music Adam and Lisa listen to? What do they think about the types of music they hear? Complete the chart.

	Type of music	Lisa's opinion	Adam's opinion
1.			
2.			
3.			

3 GRAMMAR

Double comparatives

You can use two comparatives, each preceded by *the*, in order to show how one quality or amount is linked to another. The first comparative expresses a condition for the second comparative.

The more you like to dance, **the more** you appreciate music with a Latin beat.
The more I hear a pop song on the radio, **the less** I feel like buying it.
The more exciting the soundtrack, **the better** the movie seems.
The louder the music gets, **the sooner** I feel like leaving.
The less 80s pop music I hear, **the better**.

GRAMMAR PLUS *see page 116*

A Look at the Starting Point on page 44 again. How many double comparatives can you find?

B Pair work Match the clauses to make logical statements. Then compare answers with a partner. Which statements do you agree with?

1. The more types of music you try to listen to, __c__
2. The more often you go to dance clubs, ____
3. The more companies a new artist sends a demo recording to, ____
4. The more you study the history of American popular music, ____
5. The less emphasis schools place on music, ____

a. the fewer new musicians will be developed.
b. the more you realize how much influence African music has had on it.
c. the more likely you are to enjoy a wide variety of genres.
d. the greater your chance of suffering some hearing loss.
e. the better his or her chances are of getting a recording contract.

"I agree with the first statement. Listening to lots of different genres naturally leads you to appreciate more of them."

C Complete these sentences with your own ideas. Can you add further information to clarify or support the statements you wrote?

1. The earlier children start playing music, . . .
2. The more famous a recording artist becomes, . . .
3. The catchier the melody of a pop song, . . .
4. The more expensive a musical performance is, . . .
5. The more thoughtful the song's lyrics are, . . .
6. The older I get and the more I listen to music, . . .

D Pair work Compare and discuss the sentences you wrote above. Share your opinions with the class.

"The earlier children start playing music, the better. Research suggests that music improves memory and increases attention."

"I agree. I think that sometimes we just think of math or language classes as being beneficial, but in fact, . . ."

4 VOCABULARY
Describing music

A Look at the collocations below. Match the adjectives used to describe music with their definitions.

1. a **soothing** rhythm _e_
2. a **monotonous** beat ____
3. an **exhilarating** tempo ____
4. **evocative** music ____
5. a **frenetic** pace ____
6. a **haunting** melody ____
7. **mellow** sounds ____
8. a **catchy** tune ____

a. fast and energetic, and rather uncontrolled
b. sadly beautiful and difficult to forget
c. bringing to mind a strong emotion or image
d. pleasing and easy to remember
e. relaxing, calming, and comforting
f. cool, laid-back, and smooth
g. following the same pattern; unchanging
h. making you feel very excited and happy

B Pair work Which of the adjectives from part A could you use to describe these types of sounds, music, and performances?

- a live performance by a punk rock band
- the sound of rain and howling wind
- the soundtrack to an action movie
- the sound of ocean waves
- fast-paced techno music
- classical music played by an orchestra
- soft jazz with a slow beat
- a children's nursery rhyme

VOCABULARY PLUS see page 135

5 DISCUSSION
Music everywhere

A Pair work What kind of music would you expect to hear in these places or at these events? What purpose does music serve in each situation?

- the street
- a wedding
- a clothing store
- a café
- a supermarket
- a gym
- a sports event
- a birthday party

"On the street, I would expect to hear musicians playing catchy or evocative tunes in order to convince passersby to donate some money."

B Group work What are some of the ways that music is or could be used in these fields? Discuss the benefits and drawbacks.

- education
- health care
- advertising
- entertainment

"I think music, especially if it's mellow, can be used in the classroom to focus students' attention."

"Yes, but I think people are different, and some require silence to concentrate."

6 WRITING

Compare-and-contrast essays

A compare-and-contrast essay presents the similarities and differences of two or more things. The thesis statement expresses your position on the subject, and it is followed by supporting paragraphs that discuss similarities and differences.

A Read the essay and circle the thesis statement. Then match each paragraph to the headings below. Underline the words that show comparison or contrast.

____ introduction ____ differences ____ conclusion ____ similarities

THE BEATLES VS. THE ROLLING STONES

1 Although the Beatles and the Rolling Stones have both been called the "greatest rock 'n' roll band of all time," the prize should go to the Rolling Stones. While both bands have had a huge influence on popular music, the Beatles broke up in 1970, and the Rolling Stones went on recording and performing for over 50 years.

2 Both the Beatles and the Rolling Stones began as four-member British bands that first became popular in the 1960s. The two bands released their first records within a year of each other, and both featured a pair of talented songwriters: Paul McCartney and John Lennon for the Beatles, and Mick Jagger and Keith Richards for the Rolling Stones. Like the Rolling Stones, the Beatles were famous for their cutting-edge style at the time of their debut, and both bands were known for their energetic stage performances.

3 In the beginning, the Beatles were clean-cut boys with short hair who wore suits. In contrast, the Rolling Stones had a "bad boy" image – they dressed in funky clothes and acted like rebels. One of the Beatles' first major hits was the catchy love song "I Want to Hold Your Hand," but the Stones' first big hit was a rock song called "Satisfaction." While the Beatles were pop stars, the Rolling Stones were rockers.

4 It's true that the Beatles did amazing things during the short time they were together, and their innovations are still apparent in today's music. However, the Rolling Stones were the first band to offer the world "real" rock music, and even after all these years, their music still rocks. That says it all.

B Choose two bands, singers, or musical styles to compare and contrast, and make a list of similarities and differences. Then compose a thesis statement that expresses your view.

C Write a four-paragraph essay. Make sure it has an introduction with a clear thesis statement, two paragraphs describing similarities and differences, and an effective conclusion.

D **Pair work** Take turns reading your essays. Do not read your thesis statement. Can your partner guess your point of view?

1 STARTING POINT
Music success stories

A Read about these three music success stories. Do you know these singers? Do you know how any other famous singers began their music careers?

Bruno Mars

Bruno Mars, born Peter Gene Bayot Hernández Jr., grew up in a very musical family in Hawaii. At age four, he would play with his family's band five days a week. When he was only 17, he moved to L.A. to write and produce music. At concerts, you'll see this multi-talented musician sing and play the piano or the guitar with ease.

From a very young age, Adele would perform for her mother, impersonating her favorite singers. She went to a performing arts academy in her teens, and, while there, a friend posted some of her songs online. Two years later, recording companies started noticing her. Despite her fame, Adele will still sometimes suffer from stage fright before a performance.

Adele

Rihanna

As a girl in Barbados, Robyn Rihanna Fenty would sell clothes at a street stall. She loved to sing with neighbors and friends. True talent will always be noticed. In 2003, a visiting music producer discovered her. Today, superstar Rihanna will often reinvent her look with startling new hairstyles and clothes.

B Pair work What qualities and opportunities does a person need to have in order to be a success in the popular music industry? Share your ideas with a partner.

"I think it's important to have an established person in the business take an interest in your talent and help you get your start."

2 VOCABULARY
Breaking into the business

A Look at these expressions related to show business and fame. Write them in the chart below. Compare with a partner.

be a big hit	make it big	get your big break	break into the business
be a has-been	be washed up	make a comeback	make a name for yourself
be discovered	pay your dues	be a one-hit wonder	get your foot in the door

Just starting out	Currently successful	No longer successful
	be a big hit	

B Pair work Talk about famous people you know. How did they start out? Which ones are still successful? Which ones are has-beens?

"Mark Wahlberg has really made a name for himself. He went from singer to model to Oscar-nominated actor."

VOCABULARY PLUS *see page 135*

3 GRAMMAR

Will and *would* for habits and general truths

You can use *would* to express habitual actions in the past. *Would* is more formal than *used to* and is frequently used in past narratives. *Would* needs to be clearly associated with a time in the past.

From a very young age, Adele **would** perform for her mother.

You can use *will* to express personal habits or characteristic behavior in the present.

Today, superstar Rihanna **will** often reinvent her look with startling new hairstyles and clothes.

***Will* is also used to express facts that are generally true.**

True talent **will** always be noticed.

GRAMMAR PLUS *see page 117*

A Look at the Starting Point on page 48 again. Which other habitual actions are expressed using *would* and *will*?

B Complete these sentences using the verb in parentheses and *would* or *will*.

1. In my younger days, I __*would play*__ (play) in a band at local clubs.
2. I love playing the piano. I ______________ (practice) every chance I get.
3. After he went deaf, Beethoven ______________ (compose) music in his head.
4. My son loves to play his electric guitar. Whenever he can, he ______________ (plug) it in and play a few songs.
5. When she was only 11 years old, Japanese violinist Midori Goto ______________ (perform) in front of large audiences with confidence.
6. As a young man in Britain, singer-songwriter James Morrison ______________ (gain) valuable experience by performing for people on the street.

C Read these descriptions of people. Then use your own ideas to write sentences describing their habitual actions with *would* or *will*.

1. When Ricky was a little boy, he was crazy about his violin.
   He would take it with him wherever he went.
2. Evan is really interested in learning all he can about today's top musicians.
3. Our teacher used to have lots of good ideas to pass the time on monotonous school bus trips.
4. The music Helen listened to as a teen was very different from what's popular these days.
5. The key to Jennifer's successful music career is that she teaches and performs.

D **Pair work** Complete these statements with true information. Then write a follow-up sentence using *would* or *will*. Share your answers with a partner.

1. I really enjoy listening to . . .
2. When I was young, I loved . . .
3. It's true that musicians today . . .

"I really enjoy listening to techno music. I'll listen to it when I'm feeling tired or sad, and it will always make me feel better."

4 LISTENING
Guitar blues

A **Pair work** You are going to listen to Paul, a young musician, talk to Theresa about his career. What do you think some of his concerns might be? Tell your partner.

B Now listen to the conversation between Paul and Theresa. What's Paul's biggest problem?

C Listen again. What advice does Theresa give Paul regarding each of these four areas? Complete the chart.

	Theresa's advice
1. His parents	
2. His opinion of himself	
3. His appearance	
4. The possibility of failure	

5 DISCUSSION
The secrets of success

A **Group work** Discuss the following questions with your group.

1. What are some of the ways that some actors and singers have made it big?
2. What are some of the things that successful people have in common?
3. What is your definition of *success*?

B Read the advice for success below. Choose the three pieces of advice that you think are most useful.

Advice *for* Success

- ○ 1. **Don't be afraid to dream.** You don't need to accept limitations others put on you.
- ○ 2. **Don't talk about your plans too much.** Spend that energy making things happen.
- ○ 3. **Take yourself seriously.** Pursue your dreams with conviction.
- ○ 4. **Don't try to do it all alone.** Seek out the people and resources you need.
- ○ 5. **Always appear confident** – even if you don't always feel that way inside.
- ○ 6. **Think positively.** Don't let yourself have negative thoughts for very long.
- ○ 7. **Don't be afraid to fail.** All successful people will fail – and learn a lot from it.
- ○ 8. **Dress for success.** Figure out how you need to look to get what you want.

C **Group work** Tell your group which three pieces of advice you chose. Explain why you think they are useful.

6 READING
Famous without knowing it

A Pair work How could a musician possibly become famous without knowing it? Discuss with a partner. Then read the article.

ON THE TRAIL OF SIXTO RODRIGUEZ

Sixto Rodriguez, a Mexican-American construction worker from Detroit, used to perform his songs in the city's small clubs in the late sixties. Known simply as Rodriguez, he would perform with his back to the audience. "There was something mysterious about him," says one local who saw him back then.

During that period, Rodriguez recorded and released two albums – *Cold Fact* and *Coming From Reality*. Sales, though, were small, and the albums disappeared without a trace. Since he'd never had a big hit, no one in the United States thought much more about Rodriguez after that.

But in South Africa, a bootleg copy of *Cold Fact* wound up being distributed on a small South African record label and some songs got played on the radio. Those songs became incredibly popular, and Rodriguez's reputation spread – along with the myths about him.

In those pre-Internet days, there was no information from the United States about this long-forgotten artist. Most people thought he had died, and the mystery surrounding Rodriguez just increased his incredible popularity in South Africa.

Documentary filmmaker Malik Bendjelloul stumbled on the Rodriguez story in 2006 while in Cape Town, where "every other person knew and loved Rodriguez," he recalls. "He was huge there – bigger than the Rolling Stones."

However, a decade earlier, two of his biggest South African fans, Cape Town record store owner Steve Segerman and music journalist Craig Bartholomew, had already set out to find out what had happened to Rodriguez.

The two men studied every Rodriguez lyric to establish where he might have lived and then found the producer of Rodriguez's album *Cold Fact*. Finally, the truth was revealed: Rodriguez was alive, had three adult daughters, and was still living in the same house in Detroit and doing construction work. Rodriguez knew nothing of his astonishing popularity in South Africa.

Segerman finally spoke with Rodriguez from Cape Town. The next step was for Rodriguez to perform there. He flew from the States with his daughters and was astonished to find a limousine waiting for him. On that first tour, Rodriguez played six sold-out concerts in a 5,000-seat hall. Crowds went wild, and *Cold Fact* went platinum, selling half a million copies in South Africa.

Footage of those first concerts, and the fan frenzy they inspired, can be seen in *Searching for Sugar Man*, Bendjelloul's documentary that tells the story of Rodriguez. Finally, his work will be heard widely.

Source: "Sixto Rodriguez: On the Trail of the Dylan of Detroit," by David Gritten, *The Telegraph*

B Read the article again. Are these statements true (*T*), false (*F*), or is the information not given (*NG*)? Correct the false statements to make them true.

____ 1. In the United States, Rodriguez's recordings were not commercially successful in the 1960s.

____ 2. *Cold Fact* sold more copies in the United States than *Coming From Reality* did.

____ 3. Rodriguez's songs helped Segerman and Bartholomew find the musician.

____ 4. Bendjelloul had heard about Rodriguez before he went to South Africa.

____ 5. Rodriguez was not really surprised about how he was greeted in Cape Town.

____ 6. Tickets for the first Rodriguez tour of South Africa were incredibly expensive.

C Group work How do you think instant fame affects people? Does age matter? How do you think Rodriguez's life changed after his trip to South Africa? Discuss your answers.

COMMUNICATION REVIEW

UNITS 4–6

SELF-ASSESSMENT

How well can you do these things? Choose the best answer.

I can . . .	Very well	OK	A little
▸ Describe and evaluate television shows (Ex. 1)	☐	☐	☐
▸ Take part in a discussion about movies and movie-related topics (Ex. 2)	☐	☐	☐
▸ Understand a radio program about superstitions (Ex. 3)	☐	☐	☐
▸ Describe and evaluate music and songs (Ex. 4)	☐	☐	☐
▸ Take part in a decision-making discussion about music and songs (Ex. 4)	☐	☐	☐

Now do the corresponding exercises. Was your assessment correct?

1 DISCUSSION

My kind of show

A Think of an example of each type of television show. For each show, write at least one good point about it and one change that would improve it.

Type of show	Example	Good points	Changes you'd make
game show			
reality TV show			
soap opera			
talk show			
drama series			

B **Pair work** Compare your ideas with a partner. Use sentence adverbs.

"For me, CSI *is unquestionably the best TV show ever."*

"I like it, too. Apparently, some of the episodes are based on real crimes. But one thing I'd change is . . ."

2 DISCUSSION

You have to see this!

A Think about your movie-viewing habits. Give an example for each of these topics.

1. a movie you would recommend
2. the most interesting character you've ever come across in a movie
3. a book you would like to see made, or that has already been made, into a movie
4. a movie that you would rather see in a theater than at home

B **Pair work** Discuss your ideas with a partner.

"I recommend Life of Pi. *It's so moving that it actually made me cry."*

3 LISTENING
Superstitious actors

A You are going to listen to a show about superstitions in the acting profession. Why do you think actors might be more superstitious than non-actors?

B Now listen to the program. What is the main reason Jeffrey gives for superstition among actors? Choose the correct answer.

- ☐ a. They used to feel isolated from the rest of society.
- ☐ b. They are insecure.
- ☐ c. They travel a lot.

C Listen again. Choose the theater superstition you hear in each pair.

1. ☐ a. Black cats are considered lucky.
   ☐ b. Black cats are considered unlucky.
2. ☐ a. A costume is unlucky if a cat has slept on it.
   ☐ b. A costume is unlucky unless a cat has slept on it.
3. ☐ a. The number 13 is believed to be lucky.
   ☐ b. The number 13 is believed to be unlucky.
4. ☐ a. It is unlucky to act in the play *Macbeth*.
   ☐ b. It is unlucky to say the name of the play *Macbeth*.

4 SPEAKING
Hit songs

A Pair work What are the five best songs from the last three years? Support your choices with reasons. Make a list of five songs you both agree on.

B Group work Join another pair and share your lists. Then discuss which three songs are the very best. Create a new list you all agree on and share it with the rest of the class. Is there one song that appears on all the lists?

"How do you feel about . . . ?"

"Well, the more I hear it, the more I like it. It's pretty evocative. But I'm also into music with a mellow and soothing sound. What do you think about . . . ?"

GRAMMAR PLUS

1A Phrasal verbs

Additional phrasal verbs
Separable: call off, count out, cut off, get across, hand over, pass up, take back
Inseparable: go over, hang around, live up to, look after, pick on, run out of, touch on
Intransitive: catch on, come along, come over, fall apart, show up, turn out

Certain intransitive two-word phrasal verbs, when followed by a preposition, can then take an object.

back down (from)	cut back (on)	drop out (of)	give in (to)
catch up (to)	cut down (on)	get along (with)	give up (on)
check out (of)	drop in (on)	get away (with)	look back (on)

When confronted with an argument, Mark never **backs down**.
Mark never **backs down from** an argument.

1 Underline the phrasal verb in each sentence. Is the verb separable (*S*) or inseparable (*I*)? Is it transitive (*T*) or intransitive (*NT*)? Write the correct letters.

S, T 1. The referees called the soccer match off due to heavy rain.
____ 2. Jessica asked me to come over to her house for dinner.
____ 3. Sometimes I find it hard to live up to my parents' expectations.
____ 4. Sally insulted me yesterday, but today she took back her remark.
____ 5. When entertaining, there's nothing worse than running out of food at your party.
____ 6. When Jim gave me the chance to share his apartment, I couldn't pass up the opportunity.

2 Complete the sentences with intransitive phrasal verbs and a preposition from the grammar box. Be sure to use the correct form of the verb.

1. When my grandfather and I go jogging together, I sometimes need to stop and wait for him to *catch up to* me.
2. I didn't want to try bungee jumping, but I finally ________________ the pressure from my friends and tried it. It was fun!
3. Even when you fail, a true friend will never ________________ you.
4. My friends and I are trying to ________________ the money we spend, so on Fridays we just watch TV at my house.
5. Mia's father is successful, even though he ________________ college.
6. There's a long line of people waiting to ________________ the hotel.
7. I insist on honesty; I won't let anyone ________________ lying to me.

1B Gerund and infinitive constructions

The verbs *forget*, *mean*, and *regret* can be followed by either an infinitive or a gerund. However, the meaning is significantly different in each case.

***Forget* followed by an infinitive refers to something you didn't actually do. *Forget* followed by a gerund refers to an action that you in fact did earlier.**

Marcello **forgot to meet** his best friend at the train station.

Marcello never **forgot meeting** his favorite actor.

***Mean* followed by an infinitive means "intend." In this case, *mean* is usually used in the negative or in the past tense. *Mean* followed by a gerund means "involve or necessitate."**

I **meant to visit** Sheila while I was in Hawaii, but I didn't have the chance.

Inviting Emile to the party **means inviting** Eva, too. She'd be so insulted if we didn't.

***Regret* followed by infinitives such as *inform*, *announce*, and *say* is a polite way of introducing bad news in official communication. *Regret* followed by a gerund means "be sorry for/about."**

The corporation **regrets to inform** you that all job vacancies have been filled.

Donna really **regretted missing** her best friend's wedding.

***Be* + adjective expressions are often followed by an infinitive.**

be amazed	be determined	be happy	be lucky
be ashamed	be eager	be hesitant	be ready

***Be* + adjective + preposition and verb + preposition expressions are often followed by a gerund.**

be bored with   be convinced of   be good at   be used to   be worried about
apologize for   complain about   object to   participate in   take part in   think of

1 Choose the correct form of the verb.

1. Manny forgot *to do* / *doing* his homework for English class because he had completed it over a month ago.
2. Mina didn't mean *to frighten* / *frightening* the baby with the doll.
3. Though she didn't have much, Wendy never regretted *to spend* / *spending* money on her friends.
4. I always forget *to call* / *calling* my parents, and they get really mad at me.
5. Attending my high school reunion means *to see* / *seeing* old friends as well as people I didn't like very much.
6. We regret *to announce* / *announcing* that Flight 54 has been delayed.

2 Complete the sentences with the infinitive or gerund form of the verb in parentheses.

1. Gil is really eager ___*to rekindle*___ (rekindle) his relationship with Lana.
2. I've been worried about ______________ (meet) my new college roommate.
3. I think you're really lucky ______________ (have) so many close friends.
4. Have you thought of ______________ (send) an e-card instead of mailing a card?
5. I'm ashamed ______________ (say) that my college roommate and I never reconnected.
6. I would like to apologize for ______________ (rehash) all these old issues.

2A Review of verb patterns

Here are some verbs that are used with each pattern.

a. verb + infinitive
afford, fail, hasten, learn, prepare, proceed, seek, strive
I really **strive to wear** the latest styles and trends.

b. verb + object + infinitive
advise, allow, authorize, cause, convince, encourage, instruct, permit, persuade, urge
The salesperson **convinced me to buy** a dress I knew I didn't need.

c. verb + gerund
can't help, can't see, can't stand, enjoy, get through, keep on, (not) mind, miss, postpone, risk
I **can't see paying** high prices for clothes that will be out of style in a year.

d. verb + object + preposition + gerund/noun
blame (for), dissuade (from), forgive (for), interest (in), keep (from), suspect (of), thank (for)
Can I **interest you in going** on a shopping spree with me?

1 Label the words in boldface in the text below with the correct verb pattern above.

A famous saying goes, "Clothes make the man." My mother used to say that to me because I was a sloppy dresser, and she (1) _b_ **urged me to look** my best. She'd coax me to dress better, but nothing could (2) ____ **keep me from wearing** jeans. At my high school, students never (3) ____ **failed to wear** jeans to school, and my mother always sighed and tried to (4) ____ **dissuade me from leaving** the house in my old, torn jeans. On my graduation from high school, my parents gave me my first suit and (5) ____ **advised me to "dress** for success."

Since then, I've changed quite a bit. I really (6) ____ **enjoy dressing** fashionably. I can (7) ____ **afford to wear** stylish slacks and shirts, with well-polished shoes. It's funny, but I (8) ____ **don't miss wearing** jeans one bit.

2 Complete the sentences by putting the words in parentheses in the correct order and by choosing the correct verb form. Write the letter of the pattern from the grammar box next to each sentence.

_d_ 1. I _forgave my sister for giving away_ my old laptop. (my sister / forgive / give away / for)

____ 2. I never ________________ more for quality clothes. (mind / pay)

____ 3. Harold ________________ his jacket last week. (allow / wear / me)

____ 4. Shirley ________________ her dry cleaning for another week. (pick up / postpone)

____ 5. Lydia's dad ________________ him a necktie for Father's Day. (get / her / thank / for)

____ 6. The man stole the sneakers, and then ________________ them in the mall. (wear / proceeded)

2B Cleft sentences with *what*

To emphasize the whole sentence rather than just the part following the main verb, use a cleft sentence with *what* and a form of the verb *do.*

I try to project a positive attitude.
What I try to project is a positive attitude. *(emphasizes* a positive attitude*)*
What I do is try to project a positive attitude. *(emphasizes the whole sentence)*

She complained to the waiter about the quality of the food.
What she complained about to the waiter was the quality of the food.
What she did was complain to the waiter about the quality of the food.

Cleft structures can include expressions like *the reason why*, *the thing that*, *the place where*, and *the person who.* These structures are typically used with the verb *be.*

I'm wearing sunglasses to protect my eyes.
The reason why I'm wearing sunglasses **is** to protect my eyes.

I do all my shopping at the mall.
The place where I do all my shopping **is** (at) the mall.

1 Rewrite these sentences as cleft sentences with *what* to emphasize the whole sentence.

1. The candidate showed the voters he was a trustworthy man.
   What the candidate did was show the voters he was a trustworthy man.
2. My mother shouldn't have made me wear my sister's old clothes.
3. I'm going to send all my shirts out to be dry-cleaned.
4. My friends call me at work all the time.
5. My father judges people too much by their appearance.
6. Employees should carry ID cards at all times.
7. Eleanor wore her mother's wedding dress at her own wedding.
8. Martin spilled spaghetti sauce on his shirt.
9. Sam bought a whole new wardrobe.
10. Mary is going to wear her diamond necklace to the party.

2 Rewrite these sentences as cleft sentences by starting them with the expressions in parentheses.

1. I'm wearing a tie to impress my boss. (the reason why)
   The reason why I'm wearing a tie is to impress my boss.
2. I lost my watch in the park. (the place where)
3. The office dress code changed last Friday. (the day when)
4. My dog wears a sweater because his fur is short. (the reason why)
5. I remember the intense expression on his face. (the thing that)
6. Lori keeps her jewelry under her bed. (the place where)

3A Indefinite and definite articles

In completely general statements with uncountable nouns, do not use an article before the noun. However, *the* is required when the noun is made more specific by a modifying phrase following it.
Ethics is becoming an important part of the field of genetics.
The ethics of cloning should be addressed by experts in the field.

Image is an important part of success.
The image she projected did not serve her well in court.

With certain exceptions, do not use *the* before:
countries (exceptions: *the Philippines*, *the United Arab Emirates*, *the United Kingdom*, *the United States*)
streets and cities (exception: *the Hague*)
individual lakes, bays, islands, continents, mountain peaks (exception: *the Matterhorn*)

Do use *the* before:
rivers, oceans, seas, gulfs, mountain ranges, peninsulas, deserts, forests

1 Do the nouns in these sentences require a definite article? Write *the*, or *X* if none is needed.

1. A large number of oil wells have been drilled in *the* Gulf of Mexico.
2. There is no room for ____ frivolity when discussing ____ safety of nuclear power.
3. ____ United States utilizes more genetically modified food than ____ Europe does.
4. You shouldn't expect ____ confidentiality when you upload anything to the Internet.
5. In a moment, our experimental driverless vehicle will turn right on ____ Elm Street.
6. Many people do not believe that ____ rights of animals should be protected.
7. A global warming monitoring station is located on top of ____ Mount Rutherford.
8. I think ____ human error is to blame for the majority of aircraft accidents.

2 Review the rules for articles on page 19. Then fill in the blanks with a definite article, an indefinite article, or *X* if none is needed. Sometimes more than one answer is possible.

(1) *X* Energy seems to be on everyone's mind these days. (2) ____ people are worried because they know that petroleum reserves are not infinite. It's also alarming that (3) ____ temperature of the earth seems to be rising year by year. Many scientists blame (4) ____ warming of the earth on (5) ____ burning of petroleum-based fuels.

However, there is no reason to give up (6) ____ hope, as (7) ____ alternatives are available. One example is (8) ____ wind farm, a collection of wind turbines that turn wind energy into electric power. Another example is (9) ____ hydroelectric facilities, which change (10) ____ energy created by moving water into electric power. (11) ____ hydroelectric facility on (12) ____ Paraná River in Brazil generates about 20 percent of the power used in the country. A final example is (13) ____ solar power. It is one of (14) ____ cleanest sources of energy and is attracting (15) ____ attention as well. Many countries, including (16) ____ United Arab Emirates, (17) ____ Spain, and (18) ____ India have built large solar power plants.

Lastly, it's important that we all conserve energy. Take (19) ____ moment to shut off and unplug any electrical items when you leave (20) ____ room.

3B -ing clauses

When -*ing* clauses begin a sentence, the agent of the -*ing* clause must be the subject of the main clause that follows.

Incorrect: Trying hard to fix my computer, ~~**the dog** kept staring at me~~.
(The agent of the -ing *clause seems to be* the dog.*)*
Correct: Trying hard to fix my computer, **I** noticed the dog staring at me.
(The agent of the -ing *clause and the subject of the main clause are the same.)*

Incorrect: Doing yard work, ~~**his clothes** got very dirty~~.
(The agent of the -ing *clause seems to be* his clothes.*)*
Correct: Doing yard work, **he** got dirt all over his clothes.
(The agent of the -ing *clause and the subject of the main clause are the same.)*

In addition to starting a sentence, -*ing* clauses can also follow these expressions:

have a good time	have an easy time	have fun	spend time
have a hard time	have difficulty	have problems	waste time

1 Choose the main clause that makes sense with the -*ing* clause.

1. Making strange noises, *b*
   a. I knew that my computer would crash.
   b. my computer stopped working.
2. Being technophiles, ____
   a. we're never afraid to try new gadgets.
   b. the latest gadgets always interest us.
3. Talking on her cell phone, ____
   a. the car went right through a red light.
   b. Pam didn't pay attention to her driving.
4. Quickly closing her laptop, ____
   a. Meg accidentally spilled her coffee.
   b. Meg's coffee was accidentally spilled.
5. Having studied robotics at school, ____
   a. they could explain how the robot worked.
   b. the robot was no mystery to them.

2 Combine these sentences using an expression from the grammar box to start the sentence.

1. I played video games all day Saturday. I had a good time.
   I had a good time playing video games all day Saturday.
2. My brother was shopping for cars. He had a hard time.
3. Fred constantly checks his social networking pages. He wastes a lot of time.
4. I'm attending the big technology expo next week. I'm going to have fun.
5. Nash is having difficulty. He's trying to comprehend the concept of DNA storage.
6. Norah was writing a genetic technology lecture. She spent a lot of time on it.
7. The guard used the video surveillance camera to identify the intruder. He had an easy time.
8. We were trying to follow what the scientist was saying. We were having problems.

4A Reporting clauses

In reporting clauses, verbs such as *admit*, *agree*, *announce*, *comment*, *complain*, *confess*, *disclose*, *explain*, *inform*, and *reveal* are frequently followed by an indirect object. In this case, *that* should be retained for clarity.

Several people **agreed with me that** logic, not superstition, is the best way to make decisions.
Max **explained to the teacher that** a black cat never means bad luck in his country.

The following nouns are also often used in reporting clauses. Here, too, *that* is helpful in making the meaning clear and should be retained.

accusation	assertion	comment	explanation	response
argument	claim	decision	remark	suggestion

Bill made the **assertion that** he'd have no luck at all if it weren't for bad luck.
Liliana repeated her **argument that** only foolish people believe in magic.
The class rejected Niran's **suggestion that** we cancel class on Friday the 13th.

1 Using the words in parentheses, rewrite these sentences with reporting clauses in the simple past.

1. He had an irrational fear of spiders. (Luis / admit / his friend)
   Luis admitted to his friend that he had an irrational fear of spiders.
2. Some people really are luckier than others. (Min / agree / me)
3. There are too many pigeons in the park. (many people / complain / park staff)
4. He had spent his father's lucky dollar on candy. (Marco / confess / his mother)
5. It's bad luck to step on a crack in the sidewalk. (Marcie / explain / her little sister)
6. The day he met his wife was the luckiest day of his life. (Felix / announce / his wedding guests)

2 Combine the sentences using a reporting clause with one of the nouns from the grammar box.

1. Kim accused Anna of being a superstitious person. Anna didn't agree.
   Anna didn't agree with Kim's accusation that she was a superstitious person.
2. Gianna argues that everything happens for a reason. Many people disagree.
3. Leslie asserted that superstition is based in fear. Carlos didn't understand.
4. Jae-woo decided that a trip to Las Vegas was what he needed. We were surprised.
5. Ernesto commented that hard work is more important than luck. Lily repeated what he said.
6. Hiroshi claimed he had won the chess game thanks to beginner's luck. Sandra didn't believe him.
7. Patrick remarked that Tanya probably shouldn't push her luck. Tanya ignored what he said.
8. Mr. Wang responded that actions speak louder than words. I understood him.

4B Reporting clauses in the passive

The following verbs can be used in reporting clauses in the passive.

announce	deny	maintain	reveal	suggest
confirm	estimate	observe	rumor	understand

Reporting clauses in the passive are commonly used with a variety of structures.
Simple present: It **is suggested** that passengers report anything suspicious to the driver.
Simple past: It **was** flatly **denied** that a nuclear submarine had been lost in the Arctic Ocean.
Present perfect: It **has been estimated** that the construction of Stonehenge took over 20 million hours.
Past perfect: It **had been rumored** that a monster was living in the lake.
With modals: It **couldn't be denied** that many mysteries elude scientific understanding.
With past modals: It **should have been confirmed** that the flight would be delayed.

Reporting clauses in the passive are used in written and formal English and are not common in conversation.

1 Add a reporting clause in the passive with *it* to these statements. Use the verb and the suggested structure in parentheses.

1. The lost city of Atlantis had been discovered on April Fool's Day, 1980. (announce, simple past)
   It was announced that the lost city of Atlantis had been discovered on April Fool's Day, 1980.
2. A fast-food restaurant discontinued a favorite hamburger as a publicity stunt. (reveal, present perfect)
3. Some people have a higher level of intuition than others. (understand, simple present)
4. Crop circles, patterns created by flattening crops, are a clever hoax. (can't deny, present modal)
5. The moon's pull on the earth affects the ocean tides. (maintain, simple present)
6. The politician was deceiving the nation. (should reveal, past modal)
7. A positive attitude was an important part of his cure. (observe, simple past)
8. One out of ten people falls for Internet scams every year. (estimate, past perfect)

2 Rewrite these statements with a reporting clause in the passive with *it.*

1. An unknown source maintains that the Loch Ness Monster has been sighted several times.
   It is maintained that the Loch Ness Monster has been sighted several times.
2. Archeologists have revealed that the ancient residents of Easter Island likely painted their statues.
3. Officials should have observed that there was a mysterious substance on the train floor.
4. People can't deny that ancient civilizations possessed knowledge lost to us today.
5. A newspaper has confirmed that a pack of 400 wolves was terrifying a town in Siberia.
6. The authorities have announced that 10 people on the ship got sick.

5A Sentence adverbs

To express the speaker's attitude about the entire sentence, sentence adverbs are most often located at the beginning of the sentence and set off by a comma.
Predictably, the hero of the movie won the heart of the girl.

Sentence adverbs can be used in place of longer clauses that modify a sentence.
People were amazed that the movie sold 26 million tickets on its opening weekend.
Amazingly, the movie sold 26 million tickets on its opening weekend.

Nobody was surprised that the sequel was also extremely popular.
Not surprisingly, the sequel was also extremely popular.

The following conjunctive adverbs link a sentence with a preceding idea.
accordingly consequently hence indeed meanwhile otherwise thus

The coming attractions ended and the movie began; **accordingly**, the audience fell silent.

1 Rewrite the sentences using sentence adverbs to replace the boldfaced words.

1. **It's apparent to me that** movies with clichéd storylines are still very popular.
   Apparently, movies with clichéd storylines are still very popular.
2. **It's fortunate that** there were good movies available on the 13-hour plane ride.
3. **I'm being honest when I say that** I just don't care for love stories, no matter how moving they may be.
4. **Nobody can question the fact that** many historical movies present an incorrect view of history.
5. **It was bad luck that** Carol's computer froze while she was streaming that movie.
6. **In essence**, that movie is a tale of good versus evil.
7. **If it fulfills its potential**, the Internet could be the first place all new movies are shown.
8. **It's obvious to me that** you are only pretending to have seen the movie.
9. **I'm being serious when I say that** if a movie is based on a book, always read the book first.

2 Complete the sentences with a conjunctive adverb from the grammar box. Sometimes more than one answer is possible.

1. A growing number of students are watching the movie rather than reading the assigned book. *Consequently*, there has been a decrease in the reading skills of graduating seniors.
2. At the Mainstreet Theater, you sit in front of a table to watch the movie. ______________, you are served by waiters who take your order and walk between the rows.
3. Moviegoers are prohibited from texting and talking during the movie; ______________, anyone who violates that policy will be asked to leave.
4. The most popular movie stars demand extremely high salaries; ______________ the cost of producing movies with "big names" has risen.
5. It's recommended that you buy tickets in advance; __________, you might not get a seat.

5B Such . . . that and so . . . that

In written English, *so* and *such* are most often followed by a *that* clause. However, in conversation, *so* and *such* are frequently used alone to express emphatic stress.

The host on that game show is **so** funny!
That actress plays her role **so** convincingly!
The writers of that new sitcom show **such** originality!
That was **such** a great documentary!

***So much*, *so little*, *so many*, and *so few* can also be used without a *that* clause and for emphatic stress.**

There are **so many** reality TV shows these days!
That game show gives away **so much** money!

In conversation, *much* and *little* can be used as adverbs following *so*.

Why do you watch TV **so much**? (much = *"frequently"*)
That actor is featured **so little** that I sometimes forget he's on the show. (little = *"infrequently"*)

***Much*, *little*, *many*, and *few* can also serve as pronouns for nouns.**

TV can be bad for your health. I sometimes watch so **much** (TV) my eyes hurt.
He needs more free time. He has so **little** (free time) he can't keep up with the latest TV shows.
I don't watch soap operas anymore. I've seen so **many** (soap operas) that I'm tired of them.
TV news requires reporters, but there are so **few** (reporters) that many stories aren't covered.

1 Complete these sentences with *so*, *such*, *so much*, *so little*, *so many*, or *so few*.

1. You should see the Beyoncé documentary. It's ___*so*___ interesting!
2. It's a good night for watching TV. There are ____________ new shows on!
3. Ed spent ____________ money on that TV that he can't afford a stand.
4. Turn off that program right now! I've never heard ____________ language!
5. ____________ TV shows interest Jon that he rarely watches TV.
6. Shelby works long hours. He has ____________ time for TV.

2 Complete the text with *so*, *such*, *so much*, *so little*, *so many*, or *so few*.

I've spent (1) ___*such*___ a lot of time watching reality TV that I guess I'm sort of an expert. There are (2) ____________ genres of reality TV shows that it's confusing, and the list of individual shows is (3) ____________ long nobody can remember them all.

A very popular one is about fishermen in Alaska. Those guys catch (4) ____________ seafood they fill up the boat! They catch a lot of viewers, too, with consistently high ratings and more than a few important awards. One low-rated show is about home renovations. In fact, (5) ____________ people watch it that it's going to be canceled. My favorite is about pet cloning. It's quite popular. However, it's (6) ____________ a strange show that I'm really surprised (7) ____________ people like it.

I'm really glad there are channels dedicated entirely to reality TV. Honestly, I have (8) ____________ interest in other TV genres that reality TV is all I watch!

6A Double comparatives

These structures are commonly used in double comparatives.

***The* + *more* / *less* + clause**
The more I listen to classical music, the more I appreciate it.

***The* + comparative form of adjective + clause**
The more romantic a song is, the less my brother wants to listen to it.

***The* + comparative form of adverb + clause**
The louder Mario plays his stereo, the more his neighbors complain.

***The* + *more* / *less* / *fewer* + noun / gerund + clause**
The more dancing you do, the more natural you'll feel on the dance floor.

Short double comparatives without verbs are common in conversation.
Many of them end in *the better*.
The more, the merrier!
The bigger, the better!
The sooner, the better!

1 Fill in the blanks to create appropriate double comparatives. For comparatives with adjectives or adverbs, more than one answer is possible.

1. Ricky seems to play his music loud in his car in order to get attention. ___*The louder*___ the music is, ___*the more*___ people turn their heads.
2. This song is so catchy! ________________ I listen to it, ________________ I like it.
3. The price of concert tickets has really gone up. And, ________________ the performer is, ________________ the ticket is.
4. I love soothing background music. ________________ the music is, ________________ stress I feel.
5. They play music at the baseball game to get the fans excited. ________________ the music plays, ________________ the fans yell.
6. Practice makes perfect. ____________ you practice, ____________ you will become.
7. Even age won't slow that performer down. ________________ she gets, ________________ performances she gives.

2 Complete each conversation with one of the short double comparatives without verbs from the grammar box.

1. A: When should we officially end this meeting?
   B: ____!
2. A: How many people do you think we should invite to the party?
   B: ____!
3. A: What would you like your new house to be like?
   B: ____!

6B *Will* and *would* for habits and general truths

***Used to* and *would* are both used to express habits in the past.**
Before he became a big star, Mark **used to** play music on the street for money.
Before he became a big star, Mark **would** play music on the street for money.

However, *would* cannot be used with stative verbs such as *be, have, like, live, love, mean,* and *own.*
Correct: When I was young, I **used to** have a clarinet.
Incorrect: When I was young, I ~~**would**~~ have a clarinet.

1 Complete the sentences using *would* wherever possible. If *would* is not possible, use *used to.*

1. Before Elvis made it big, he ___*would*___ sing with his family on the front porch of his house in Tupelo, Mississippi.
2. I ____________ own a violin that my uncle gave me for my birthday. I don't know where it is now.
3. Since the young Beethoven loved nature, he ____________ take long walks along the banks of the Rhine River.
4. That performer ____________ be washed up, but he has since made a remarkable comeback.
5. Before he was discovered by a Hollywood talent scout, that singer ____________ regularly announce local sports events on the radio.
6. Café La Fortuna in New York City, where John Lennon ____________ like to have coffee and read the newspaper, closed down in 2008.
7. In the 1990s, Pavarotti ____________ perform as part of The Three Tenors with José Carreras and Plácido Domingo.
8. In high school, Madonna ____________ love to dance and ____________ always get excellent grades.
9. Although my family wasn't wealthy, we ____________ own a concert-quality grand piano.

2 Complete the paragraph using the correct form of the verb in parentheses. Use *would* or *will* for habits and general truths wherever possible.

Music has played an important role in my life since I was very young. When I was a boy, our family (1) ___*would sit*___ (sit) on the green lawn in the center of town on Saturday nights listening to the town band. Between songs, I (2) ____________ (like) to talk to the musicians about their instruments, which fascinated me. I (3) ____________ (ask) them if I could play their trumpets and clarinets, and they (4) ____________ (say) no in as gentle a way as they could. Who could have imagined that I would become an instrument maker? I've got my own family now. On warm Saturdays, I (5) ____________ (take) them down to the center of town to listen to the town band. And, every time we go, my own son (6) ____________ (bother) the musicians with questions and requests. After all, like father, like son!

VOCABULARY PLUS

1A Adjectives and verbs to describe friendship

Use the verb or adjective form from each pair in the box to complete the conversations.

admire	clash	empathize	endure	harmonize
admirable	clashing	empathetic	enduring	harmonious

1. A: My dad has been friends with Ahmet since they were roommates in college, and they still get together once a month.

   B: I really ___*admire*___ that! They must get along really well!

2. A: Teresa listens to her friends when they have problems and makes a real effort to understand their feelings.

   B: It sounds like she's ________________. In my opinion, that's an admirable quality.

3. A: Whenever I'm with Jake, we get into a fight about something ridiculous.

   B: It's too bad you two always ________________. Some friends bring out the worst in us.

4. A: My parents get along really well. On the rare occasion they have an issue, they try to discuss it rationally and reach a fair compromise.

   B: It's good they have a ________________ relationship. They must be great role models.

5. A: Some psychologists think that only people with similar personalities form strong, long-lasting friendships.

   B: I'm not sure I agree. I can think of lots of people with different personalities who have ________________ friendships. Look at us! We've been friends for over 20 years.

1B *re-* verbs

Use the correct form of five more verbs from the box to replace the underlined mistakes.

rebuild	recall	reconnect	redefine	rehash	rekindle	replace	resurface

1. Emil and Lydia attended the same school many years ago. Recently, they found each other on a social networking site and replaced their friendship. ___*rekindled*___
2. We hadn't seen Ian in class for days and were getting worried. He finally rehashed this morning and said he'd been called away to a family emergency. ________________
3. If I can't reconnect the last time I saw a friend, I can usually find that information by using the calendar function on my tablet. ________________
4. It's annoying when Jack resurfaces the same old arguments. He repeats the same points over and over again, hoping that we'll finally agree with him. ________________
5. Rachel and Yumi had a huge argument and stopped speaking to each other. Now, they've both apologized and are trying to recall their damaged friendship. ________________
6. Smartphones let us send texts and photos, locate friends, and update our status on social networking sites. They've rebuilt how we communicate. ________________

2A Adjectives to describe style

Cross out the word or phrase that does not fit the meaning of the sentence.

1. Fashion design students are up on the latest trends and always look so *chic / stylish / sloppy*.
2. The fashion photographer has a low opinion of people who always wear old jeans and T-shirts no matter the occasion. He thinks they're *frumpy / sloppy / elegant*.
3. The top women executives in that corporation favor beautifully tailored jackets and dresses. They all have *a classic / a quirky / an elegant* look.
4. On some airlines, the flight attendants wear well-designed uniforms that are functional yet *fashionable / retro / chic*.
5. The lawyers in my firm generally wear conservative suits to work, but on weekends, they often wear *functional / trendy / flashy* clothes to company parties.
6. The band members wear vintage jackets, ripped black jeans, and red sneakers. They're trying to achieve a look that's *stuffy / funky / quirky*.

2B Adjectives to describe outward appearance

Choose the correct words to complete the conversations.

1. A: I was watching that new British drama on TV last night. My favorite character is the college professor. He seems intelligent and looks *dignified / innocent* in his dark suit and neatly trimmed beard.

   B: I saw that show, too. I really like the psychologist. You can tell by his friendly, open personality that he's really *intense / trustworthy*.

   A: One character I dislike is the opera singer. She's always sneaking around and looks quite *sinister / sympathetic* in her dark sunglasses and black scarf.

2. A: Did you see the portraits at the exhibit? That general has a reputation as a great leader, but looked almost too confident in that photo. He seemed *arrogant / intellectual*.

   B: I agree. Did you see the photo of the fashion model? I think of her as being sophisticated, but in that photo, she looked sweet and *smug / innocent*.

   A: The photographer definitely has a knack for capturing personalities. I loved his shot of the artist who lives alone on a mountain. I thought she looked pretty *eccentric / sympathetic* hiking in that quirky hat and long dress.

3A Adjectives to discuss technology-related issues

Choose the best words to complete the text.

Technology does amazing things to improve our lives, but there are some things that we should keep in mind. We love all the cool things our smartphones can do, but do you think it's (1) *unethical / hazardous / prudent* to upgrade our phones every six months just to get a few more features? Aren't there more worthwhile ways to spend our money? Also, phones are made of plastic, metal, chemicals, and other potentially (2) *audacious / confidential / hazardous* materials, so we have to recycle or dispose of old devices carefully.

Another concern is electronic banking. It's certainly convenient to pay bills online, but many people worry about keeping financial information (3) *confidential / problematic / unethical*. It seems like no matter how complex our passwords are, (4) *frivolous / audacious / confidential* hackers are always able to break into our accounts – and they rarely get caught. We should track down these (5) *unethical / prudent / frivolous* tech wizards and hire them to be our security experts!

3B Collocations to express different attitudes

Combine words from the boxes to complete the sentences. Some of the prepositions are used more than once.

aware	fed up	intimidated	knowledgeable	leery	reliant

about	by	of	on	with

1. As a security expert, Mia is *knowledgeable about* using fingerprint and facial recognition systems instead of passwords.
2. Ryan is observant and notices things that most of us would miss. When he walks around our city, he's highly ________________ surveillance cameras that record people's activities.
3. My father-in-law is skeptical about most things and is especially ________________ people who offer get-rich-quick schemes. He prefers to make money by working hard and making prudent investments.
4. Jana is in her 80s now and has become increasingly ________________ her daughters to help around the house and drive her to appointments.
5. The teenagers I know think most advertising is annoying and are becoming really ________________ pop-up ads appearing on their smartphones all the time.
6. Our manager criticizes our work and often loses his temper. We sometimes feel ________________ him, but we're not sure how to improve the situation.

4A Expressions with *luck*

Use the phrases in the box to correct the underlined mistakes in the sentences.

bad luck	no such luck	the best of luck
beginner's luck	pushing his luck	the luck of the draw

1. As soon as Mei finished writing her paper, her computer crashed, and she lost all her work. That was beginner's luck! *bad luck*
2. It's dangerous for Todd to ride his motorcycle without a helmet. He hasn't had an accident yet, but he's out of luck. ________________
3. Nico will start his new job at the engineering firm tomorrow. I wished him the luck of the draw. ________________
4. Our favorite band was playing at the Village Jazz Club. I had hoped to get tickets, but best of luck. The performance was completely sold out. ________________
5. Did you hear about the woman who bought a valuable antique vase for five cents at her first online auction? That was truly a case of pushing her luck! ________________
6. Jeff had to move to a new apartment this month. By coincidence, there was an apartment available where his best friend lives. Talk about no such luck! ________________

4B Adjectives to describe truth and fabrication

Choose the correct words to complete the conversation.

Marla: Why are you reading that silly magazine? You know that most of those stories are (1) *conceivable* / *dubious* / *credible* at best.

Chad: But I enjoy making fun of the articles! Look at this crazy story about a man who saw an upside-down rainbow. Everyone knows that a rainbow's arc is at the top. It sounds pretty (2) *fishy* / *plausible* / *conceivable* to me.

Marla: Well, actually, I recently read in a science journal that an upside-down rainbow can occur. There's even a scientific name for it. So I think that story is (3) *iffy* / *misleading* / *well-founded* after all.

Chad: Really? Well, OK, here's a story about glowing green mushrooms. It's reported that if you put one on a newspaper in a dark room, it would give off so much light that you could read the words! This story sounds (4) *credible* / *phony* / *convincing* to me. I've never heard of anything like that.

Marla: But jellyfish and fireflies give off light, so why do you think it's (5) *far-fetched* / *convincing* / *misleading* for mushrooms to glow?

Chad: Well, I haven't see any (6) *fishy* / *convincing* / *dubious* evidence that glowing plants exist. But now that you say that, it does make me wonder.

Marla: Yeah, maybe that "silly magazine" isn't so silly!

5A Adjectives to describe movies

Cross out the word that does not fit the meaning of each sentence.

http://www.cup.org/bigcitycritic

Here are today's film reviews from our Big City Critic:

Mystery of the Purple Fox is set in a beautiful forest, and the actors are very talented. Unfortunately, it was easy to guess how the movie would end in the first five minutes because the story was (1) ~~*riveting*~~ / *predictable* / *formulaic*. This director's work in the past has been (2) *clichéd* / *inspiring* / *engrossing*, so I was disappointed to see such (3) *predictable* / *touching* / *mediocre* work in this film.

Glacier Meltdown is a documentary about how icebergs are melting at an alarming rate, causing the world's sea levels to rise. It was (4) *engrossing* / *riveting* / *formulaic* to see the gorgeous ice formations, but it was depressing to learn how quickly they are disappearing. It was (5) *inspiring* / *mediocre* / *moving* to watch the scientists endure dangerous conditions and severe weather as they examined the glaciers.

5B Types of TV programs

Choose the true statement for each sentence.

1. This season's most popular show has a complicated plot and characters that are always facing romantic problems and personal disasters.
   - ☐ a. This season's most popular show is a sketch comedy show.
   - ☐ b. This season's most popular show is a sports program.
   - ☐ c. This season's most popular show is a soap opera.

2. This new program features fashion stylists who pick out clothing for celebrities for important events. Viewers get to see them in action as they work.
   - ☐ a. The stylists are participants on a game show.
   - ☐ b. The stylists are stars of a reality TV show.
   - ☐ c. The stylists are hosts on a talk show.

3. The star of this show is a chef who demonstrates how to prepare exotic dishes from all over the world.
   - ☐ a. The chef stars in a sitcom about a restaurant.
   - ☐ b. The chef prepares unusual dishes on a cooking show.
   - ☐ c. The chef gives reports about food on a news program.

4. This show features animated characters. Dee the Dinosaur is the smart one. Fritz the Frog is silly and funny.
   - ☐ a. Dee and Fritz are characters in a cartoon.
   - ☐ b. Dee and Fritz are reality TV stars.
   - ☐ c. Dee and Fritz are the subjects of a documentary.

6A Collocations to describe music

Use the best two phrases from each box to complete the conversations.

an exhilarating tempo	the mellow sounds	the monotonous beat

Ann: I really enjoy listening to hip-hop music. I think it has (1) *an exhilarating tempo*.

Ben: Call me old-fashioned, but I actually prefer (2) ______________ of slow jazz.

a catchy tune	a frenetic pace	a soothing rhythm

Liz: When I work, I usually have classical music playing in the background. It has (3) ______________ that helps me stay calm.

Rob: I need to feel energized when I work, so I listen to rap. It has (4) ______________ that keeps me going.

a catchy tune	a haunting melody	an exhilarating tempo

Ted: I enjoy songs that are pleasant and easy to remember. There's something very satisfying about singing along with (5) ______________.

Jen: Oddly enough, I prefer evocative music that sounds sad. Folk music often has (6) ______________ that is hard to forget.

6B Idioms used in the entertainment industry

Match the correct words to complete the sentences.

1. Vanessa is a talented young actress who's auditioning to get her first part in a movie. She's trying to be *d*.
2. My favorite band retired years ago, but I just heard it's making ____. The band is playing at Music Hall next month.
3. If you're starting out as a comedian and want to get ____, you should try out your material in comedy clubs.
4. Maya's first song was at the top of the charts last year. She's working hard on new music because she doesn't want to be ____.
5. That blues guitarist used to be a popular musician. Unfortunately, he's not getting any club dates, and he seems to be ____.
6. To succeed as a dancer, you usually have to pay ____ in the chorus line and work hard for years before you're noticed.
7. That actor is ____ on the new television series. The network just signed him to a huge multi-year contract.

a. a one-hit wonder
b. a comeback
c. washed up
d. discovered
e. your foot in the door
f. your dues
g. a big hit

Credits

Illustration credits

Jo Goodberry: 12, 103
Paul Hostetler: 22, 23, 64, 101
Kim Johnson: 3, 26, 36, 65
Dan McGeehan: 41, 56, 84
Rob Schuster: 72, 87
Koren Shadmi: 9, 17, 53, 83
James Yamasaki: 28, 86

Photography credits

Back cover: (*clockwise from top center*) ©Leszek Bogdewicz/Shutterstock, ©Wavebreak Media/Thinkstock, ©Blend Images/Alamy, ©limpido/Shutterstock; **2** ©George Doyle/Thinkstock; **5** ©Davide Mazzoran/Thinkstock; **6** (*left to right*) ©Corbis/SupersStock, ©Jeff Greenberg/Alamy, ©Blend Images/Alamy; **8** ©Corbis/SuperStock; **10** (*top to bottom*) ©Coprid/Shutterstock, ©Neamov/Shutterstock, ©Barghest/Shutterstock, ©robert_s/Shutterstock, ©mama_mia/Shutterstock; **11** ©Ira Berger/Alamy; **13** ©alexnika/Thinkstock; **14** ©Fuse/Thinkstock; **15** ©Cultura Limited/SuperStock; **16** (*clockwise from top left*) ©Dimitrios Kambouris/Getty Images, ©Alberto E. Rodriguez/Getty Images, ©Jeffrey Mayer/WireImage/Getty Images, ©Vittorio Zunino Celotto/Getty Images; **18** (*left to right*) ©Krzysztof Gawor/Getty Images, ©Science Photo Library – SCIEPRO/Getty Images, ©Eric Isselée/Thinkstock; **19** ©EVERETT KENNEDY BROWN/epa/Corbis; **20** ©Beyond/SuperStock; **21** ©Gilles Podevins/Science Photo Library/Corbis; **24** ©Europics/Newscom; **25** ©Newspix/Getty Images; **27** (*clockwise from top left*) ©Christin Gilbert/agefotostock/SuperStock, ©al_ter/Thinkstock, ©Franck Boston/Thinkstock, ©GregC/Thinkstock, ©Nathan Allred/Thinkstock, ©Comstock/Thinkstock; **29** ©Photimageon/Alamy; **31** (*top to bottom*) ©Stockbyte/Thinkstock, ©Mykola Velychko/Thinkstock, ©Jupiterimages/Thinkstock, ©Valeriy Lebedev/Thinkstock; **32** (*clockwise from top left*) ©Jupiterimages/Thinkstock, ©Maksim Kabakou/Thinkstock, ©Elnur Amikishiyev/Thinkstock, ©Paul Poplis/Getty Images, ©guy harrop/Alamy; **33** ©Eric Staller/Splash News/Newscom; **34** ©GERARD CERLES/Getty Images; **35** ©MANAN VATSYAYANA/Getty Images; **38** ©I love images/SuperStock; **39** ©AF archive/Alamy; **42** ©Digital Vision/Thinkstock; **43** (*top to bottom*) ©courtesy of One Day on Earth, ©courtesy of One Day on Earth, ©courtesy of One Day on Earth; **44** ©OJO Images/SuperStock; **45** ©RichardBaker/Alamy; **46** ©Fernando Garcia-Murga/AgeFotostock; **47** (*left to right*) ©Fox Photos/Getty Images, ©Dave J Hogan/Getty Images; **48** (*left to right*) ©Kevin Winter/Getty Images, ©John Shearer/Getty Images, ©Chris McGrath/Getty Images; **49** ©Stanislav Tiplyashin/Thinkstock; **50** ©Jack Hollingsworth/Thinkstock; **51** ©Red Box Films/ZUMA Press/Newscom; **52** ©CBS/Getty Images; **54** ©Exactostock/SuperStock; **57** ©Wavebreakmedia Ltd/Thinkstock; **58** (*left to right*) ©Jose Luis Pelaez Inc/Blend Images/Alamy, ©Image Source/Alamy, ©David Litschel/Alamy; **59** ©Sergey Mikhailov/Thinkstock; **62** (*clockwise from top left*) ©Iryna Rasko/Shutterstock, ©Nastco/Thinkstock, ©Jupiterimages/Thinkstock, ©Ilya Shapovalov/Shutterstock; **63** ©james turner/Alamy; **66** (*left to right*) ©Art Directors & TRIP/Alamy, ©Raine Vara/Alamy, ©Raymond Boyd/Getty Images; **67** ©John Wynn/Thinkstock; **69** ©Photos 12/Alamy; **70** (*clockwise from top left*) ©Presselect/Alamy, ©Jean-Louis Atlan/Corbis, ©Rick Friedman/Corbis, ©Paris Match/Getty Images; **71** ©Photo by Adam Scull/Newscom; **73** ©Image Source/Getty Images; **74** ©Brad Perks Lightscapes/Alamy; **75** ©Getty Images/Agefotostock; **76** ©David De Lossy/Thinkstock; **77** ©STAN HONDA/Getty Images; **78** (*left to right*) ©Purestock/Thinkstock, ©Flirt/SuperStock, ©iStock/Thinkstock; **79** (*left to right*) ©iStock Collection/Thinkstock, ©Mitchell Kranz/Shutterstock, ©Fuse/Thinkstock; **80** (*left to right*) ©Tim Mosenfelder/Getty Image News/Getty Images, ©AFP/Getty Images; **82** ©Khakimullin Aleksandr/Shutterstock; **85** ©Tom Briglia/Getty Images; **88** (*left to right*) ©Elliot & Fry/Getty Images, ©Nick Harvey/WireImage/Getty Images, ©Michael Tran/FilmMagic/Getty Images; **90** (*clockwise from top left*) ©Christian Alminana/WireImage/Getty Images, ©L. Busacca/WireImage/Getty Images, ©Valerie Macon/Getty Images, ©Michael Kovac/WireImage/Getty Images, ©John Parra/WireImage/Getty Images; **91** ©Ian Gavan/Getty Images; **92** (*top to bottom*) ©iStock Collection/Thinkstock, ©iStock Collection/Thinkstock, ©iStock Collection/Thinkstock, ©Blend Images/Shutterstock, ©Siri Stafford/Thinkstock, ©gulfimages/SuperStock; **93** ©Jacek Sopotnicki/Thinkstock; **94** ©itanistock/Alamy; **95** ©VMAA/ZOB WENN Photos/Newscom; **96** (*clockwise from top right*) ©Bryan Smith/ZUMAPRESS/Newscom, ©YOSHIKAZU TSUNO/AFP/Getty Images/Newscom, ©Andrew Hasson/Photoshot/Getty Images; **100** ©Comstock Images/Thinkstock; **102** ©mediaphotos/Thinkstock; **105** (*left to right*) ©Jacob Wackerhausen/Thinkstock, ©Suprijono Suharjoto/Thinkstock, ©Chace & Smith Photography/Fuse Collection/Thinkstock; **131** ©mangostock/Thinkstock; **133** ©Mark A Schneider/Getty Images; **135** ©Blend Images/SuperStock; **136** ©George Doyle/Thinkstock; **138** ©William Curch – Summit42.com/Getty Images; **140** ©Agefotostock/SuperStock

Text credits

The authors and publishers acknowledge the following sources of copyright material and are grateful for the permissions granted. While every effort has been made, it has not always been possible to identify the sources of all the material used, or to trace all copyright holders. If any omissions are brought to our notice, we will be happy to include the appropriate acknowledgments on reprinting.

9 Adapted from "How Social Media 'Friends' Translate Into Real-Life Friendships" by Terri Thornton, *Mediashift*, July 13, 2011. Reproduced with permission of Mediashift, PBS; **16** Adapted from "Judging Faces Comes Naturally" by Jules Crittenden, *Boston Herald*, September 7, 1997. Reproduced with permission of the Boston Herald; **17** Adapted from "Overcoming a Bad First Impression" by Susan Fee, Professional Clinical Counselor, www.susanfee.com. Reproduced with permission of Susan Fee; **25** Adapted from "Family: I Unplugged My Kids" by Melissa McClements, *The Guardian*, January 1, 2011. Copyright © Guardian News & Media Ltd 2011; **35** Adapted from "Do Good-luck Charms Really Work in Competitions?" by Alex Hutchinson, *The Globe and Mail*, October 18, 2010. Reproduced with permission of Alex Hutchinson; **43** Adapted from "'One Day On Earth' Debuts Worldwide, Offers Time Capsule Of Our Lives" by Mark Johanson, *International Business Times*, April 21, 2012. Reproduced with permission of International Business Times; **51** Adapted from "Sixto Rodriguez: On the Trail of the Dylan of Detroit" by David Gritten, *The Telegraph*, June 14, 2012. Copyright © Telegraph Media Group Limited 2012; **61** Adapted from "Living the Simple Life – and Loving It" by Julia Duin, *The Washington Times*, January 5, 1996. Copyright © 1996 The Washington Times LLC. This reprint does not constitute or imply any endorsement or sponsorship of any product, service, company or organization. License # 37237; **69** Adapted from "Word-of-Mouth Marketing: We All Want to Keep Up with the Joneses" by Martin Lindstrom, www.martinlindstrom.com, September 21, 2011. Reproduced with permission of Martin Lindstrom; **77** From "A Summer Job That Promises Nature Walks for Pay" by Cara Buckley, *The New York Times*, August 13, 2008. Copyright © 2008 The New York Times. All rights reserved. Used by permission and protected by the Copyright Laws of the United States. The printing, copying, redistribution, or retransmission of this Content without express written permission is prohibited; **80** Adapted from *Schaum's Quick Guide to Great Presentation Skills* by Melody Templeton and Suzanne Sparks Fitzgerald, published by McGraw-Hill, 1999. Copyright © 1999 by the McGraw-Hill Companies, Inc.; **87** Adapted from "Slang Abroad" by Ben Falk, *The Daily Colonial*, April 1, 2006. Reproduced with permission; **95** Adapted from "Leading Questions" by Alison Benjamin, *The Guardian*, March 28, 2007. Copyright © Guardian News & Media Ltd 2007; **103** Adapted from *Job Savvy: How to Be a Success at Work Fifth Edition* by LaVerne L. Ludden, published by JIST Publishing, 2012. Reproduced with permission of JIST Publishing.

Answers

Page 32, Exercise 1B: Story 2 is false.
Page 34, Exercise 5B: They are all hoaxes.
Page 84, Exercise 2A: before, Are you OK?, See you later, excellent, great, tonight